How to Write a Hit Song

ALSO BY MOLLY-ANN LEIKIN:

How to Be a Hit Songwriter

Molly-Ann Leikin's Master Class in Songwriting (MP3 Version)

5TH EDITION

How to Write
a Hit Song

By Molly-Ann Leikin

HAL•LEONARD®

Applause Theatre & Cinema Books
33 Plymouth Street, Suite 302
Montclair, NJ 07042
Phone: (973) 337-5034
Fax: (973) 337-5227
Email: info@applausepub.com
Internet: www.applausepub.com

Trade Book Division Editorial Offices
33 Plymouth Street, Suite 302
Monclair, NJ 07042

Printed in the United States of America

Book design by UB Communications

Library of Congress Cataloging-in-Publication Data is available upon request.

ISBN 978-1-4234-4198-4

www.halleonard.com

Contents

Preface

Songwriting is the most glorious and terrible thing I know. It is the former when I'm smitten with a magical idea, and I'm happy to let it keep me awake all night. The thunder pumping through my veins stimulates me to stretch my abilities, to struggle to perfect and pamper my new song like a beloved child.

Then there are days when I'm stuck on a particular song, or when everybody seems to reject what I've written and I feel as inconsequential as a wad of dirty chewing gum someone's trying to scrape off his Gucci shoe. As devastating as it feels, and as hard as I may fall, somehow I always forget the negative side of songwriting the next time I get an idea. The thunder starts pumping again. I pick up my pen, and I'm home.

Writing makes me feel whole and substantial in a way nothing else does. When I hear my songs on the radio or online and see them listed on the charts, I feel a great sense of triumph. As for the songs that are still in the drawer and never made it to the radio, I cherish them, too, and maybe even love them a little more. The awards on my walls remind me that I made the right choices after all at the crossroads of my life, where I walked right by the signs pointing to the safe, familiar places and headed instead into the uncharted forests, singing.

Acknowledgments

My gratitude
with sour cream-cinnamon-raisin coffee cake,
nuts optional,
to:

All the Mollys, Rita Blumstein, Jeff Bosset, Bruce Broughton, Representative Lois Capps, John Carter, Nicole Sherwood Cavendish, John Cerullo, Godwin Chu, Stephen L. Cohn, Sandy Cook, downward-facing dog, 805 Deli, Melissa Etheridge, the Four Seasons Biltmore Hotel-Montecito, Judith M. Girard, Judy Harris, Ichiban Sushi, Fred Klein, Josh Leopold, Bernadette Malavarca, Tim McGraw, Marguerite Paradis, Dan Rosenbaum, David M. Ross, the Santa Barbara Symphony, Robert A. Schuller, Brad Smith, Johnny Umeda, Carrie Underwood, Via Vai pizza margherita, and Peter Quay Wright.

 # Introduction

I am a hit songwriter. My house is full of gold and platinum records, plus an Emmy nomination. I've written themes and songs for dozens and dozens of TV shows and movies, including *Eight Is Enough* and *Violet,* which won an Oscar. Over a period of ten years, I was a staff writer for three major music publishers in Hollywood and taught songwriting at UCLA, where I created the singer/songwriter workshop. More recently, I was a *Eurovision* finalist. For those of you who are not familiar with that competition, *Eurovision* is like *American Idol,* but in Europe, where instead of only one country, the competition is from forty-two.

I remember when I used to dream of being a hit songwriter. I wrote all day and rewrote all night. I ached to hear my songs on the air and wanted nothing else. In spite of the mocking voices telling me the odds were too great and I'd never make it, something kept urging me on. Someday I knew I'd get what I was after.

And I did.

People have asked me repeatedly if I'm from a musical family. I have to answer this way. My paternal grandfather, Louis Leikin, was born in Russia at a time when young men were drafted into the army. So when male babies were born, their births were not registered. My grandfather was fifteen when the government finally caught up with him. Arriving for his physical, he told the authorities he was a virtuoso violinist and should be in the army orchestra.

Unfortunately on audition day, Grampa Louie appeared with his arm in a sling, but was so passionate in convincing the army of his virtuosity they accepted him without an audition.

A few weeks later, the orchestra was touring near the Polish border. Removing his cast and leaving behind the violin he never *did* know how to play, Grampa Louie escaped. So if you ask me if I'm from a musical family, I'd have to say, not really...

The closest I came to having a relative even remotely connected to show business was my uncle Harold, who was really in the meat business but who gave the farm report every weekday at 6 A.M. on the country station in Ottawa, Canada.

I became a hit songwriter because I wanted to be one. I was driven. I would accept nothing less. I had to do this or die. If *you* have that same fire burning in you, read on, and I'll show you how I did it—how the pros do it—and how *you* can do it, too.

As a songwriting consultant in California, I work with clients of all ages and levels of musical and lyrical ability. I'm proud to tell you that some of my clients have their songs on the air right now. One was nominated for a Grammy, another won an Emmy, and as of this writing, 5,028 of my clients have placed their songs in movies, in TV shows, in soundtracks, in commercials, and on CDs. Maybe next year at this time it'll be your turn. My clients know that consulting with me is as important to their success as that new software, because without a great song, all the technical wizardry available to them is meaningless. A number-one hit song can earn its writer and publisher $250,000 a week, every week it's number one, and $250,000 a year every year after that for the writer's whole life, plus seventy years. Somebody has to write the hits. It might as well be you.

How to Write a Hit Song

1

Song Structure—
The Lyric

Some of you write words and music. Some write lyrics exclusively, and some others compose only melodies. To be successful song-writers, it's important for you to know how to structure the whole song, not just the part you create. So if you're a composer, don't skip over the chapter on lyrics. And, lyricists, pay close attention to the chapter on melody. You may think you don't need to know it, but you *do*. Someday your collaborator may be stuck and will need your help.

♪ THE LYRIC

A contemporary hit song is usually three to three and a half minutes long. Every one of them, whether written by Fergie, Keith Urban, or Maroon 5, has a specific structure: a music and lyrical pattern that repeats.

A hit song needs focus. We have to know immediately what it is about. Each line of lyric in your song should relate to the title, adding something to embellish and enhance our understanding of the subject. If you were writing a song about shoes, you'd include ideas about laces, patent leather, sneakers, cowboy boots, soles, scruffs, worn-down heels, sizes, corns, bunions, high-heels, etc. You wouldn't suddenly throw in something about a lawn mower unless the shoe was mutilated by one.

When deciding what to write about, find a theme and let us know what the song is going to be about in the first line. Stick to the same theme all the way through to the end. If you were watching a movie about a boxer who gets a shot at the title, nearly every scene and line of dialogue in that story would have to do with the man's quest for victory. The film wouldn't wander off on a tangent about things to do with string. It would remain focused on its original theme. Your songs have to be focused, too.

Exercise

Take a clean sheet of paper. Write the words "little red schoolhouse" at the top. Then list every picture or feeling those words evoke in you. Ask yourself fifty to a hundred questions like these:

1. Is the school old or new?
2. In what state is it located?
3. Is it in the country or in the city?
4. How big is it?
5. Does it need paint? If so, where?
6. What season is it?
7. Is there a weather vane?
8. Is there a bell? What kind?
9. Is the school on a hill?
10. What century is it?
11. What time of day is it?
12. Are there any animals nearby? If so, what kind? Living? Stuffed?
13. Are there any flowers and trees? If so, what kind and what color?
14. Are there steps into the school?
15. Are there children outside?
16. What are the children doing?
17. What are the children wearing? Describe every detail of their appearance-from haircuts to frayed collars to shoe laces.
18. How old are the children?
19. Are they happy? If not, why?
20. What is remarkable about the sky above the school?
21. What kind of desks are inside? Are they new?
22. If not, is anything carved on them?
23. Do you hear anything? Smell anything?
24. Is the teacher old or young? A man or a woman?

You could continue listing information about this little red schoolhouse for hours, creating a picture, embellishing it, refining it. Your picture has colors in it, which heightens the impact because it is easier to visualize. I chose the concept of a little red schoolhouse because everyone has seen one, whether it was on television, in the movies, or in real life. And everybody can list the details of what his particular building looks like. Most of my clients say it is similar to the one on the television show *Little House on the Prairie*. But another writer, who is from New York City, said that his was in Greenwich Village. Two brothers said the teacher was a very strict nun, while my next client told me her teacher was a handsome young man with a beard. It doesn't matter that we see the picture differently, as long as we see something. And we do.

If you were going to write a song about this little red schoolhouse, you would choose the information you wanted to use from the long list of possibilities you've created as a resource for yourself. You're not just sitting with a blank page trying to squeeze something out of your brain. You have a lot of choices of ideas, feelings, and pictures to include in your song from the research you've just done. And that's half the work completed right there.

I do this exercise with all my new clients. It's an excellent way of showing them how to organize their thoughts. It proves to my writers who claim to be unable to write lyrics or think they aren't capable of writing visually that they *are*, particularly if they start with a strong title, preferably one with a picture in it. This exercise shows lyricists how to keep digging for more information and make their images as specific and detailed as possible. To me, songs are *ear paintings*, and you have to make them vivid. This is the decade of dazzle. There are lots of distractions for your audience. If you want to "hook" a listener, build irresistibility into your songs. Pictures help you do that.

When you have an idea for a new song, do the exercise just as you did with "little red schoolhouse." List everything that's pertinent and collect information by asking yourself fifty to a hundred questions about the idea. If you can't list anything that goes with it, the chances are you either haven't thought it through carefully enough or your subject isn't big enough to warrant a whole song.

♪ SONG FORM

Most contemporary hit songs have two distinct lyrical and musical sections that are repeated at least once. They are the verse, called the A section, and the chorus, called the B section. There is a third part known as the bridge, or C section. The song form almost all contemporary hits on any chart follow is verse/chorus, verse/chorus, bridge/chorus. A song without a chorus is like a house without a kitchen. Nobody buys a house without a kitchen; nobody sings a song without a chorus. Leikin's law is give them what they want.

"I Need to Wake Up" by Melissa Etheridge won the Academy Award for Best Original Song.

I NEED TO WAKE UP
by Melissa Etheridge

Have I been sleeping
I've been so afraid of crumbling
Have I been careless
Dismissing all the important rumblings
Take me where I am supposed to be
To comprehend the things that I can't see ('cause)

CHORUS:
I need to move
I need to wake up
I need to change
I need to shake up
I need to speak out
Something's gotta break up
I've been asleep
And I need to wake up now

And as a child
I danced like it was 1999
My dreams were wild
The promise of this new world would be mine
Now I'm throwing off the carelessness of youth
To listen to an inconvenient truth (that)

CHORUS

BRIDGE:
I am not an island

I am not alone

I am my intentions trapped here in this flesh and bone

CHORUS

© 2007 Songs of Ridge Road. Used by permission.

The lyric is about someone who has been completely oblivious to the earth's ecological problems. She knows she's been irresponsible but wants to face and understand the dilemma.

The solution is in every syllable of the lyric in the chorus, from "I need to move" to the last line of the section, "I need to wake up now."

The story continues as Melissa remembers being young, carefree, and untamed, but now she wants to step up and become a responsible citizen. In the bridge, she says hers isn't an isolated case, and it's time to put her actions where her heart is, doing something to fix the problem. There isn't a wasted syllable in the lyric. It is tight, succinct, passionate, and a call to action to save our planet.

While most of us won't get a phone call from Vice President Al Gore asking us to write a little something for his slideshow, Melissa Etheridge got that call and wrote that song. The event was being filmed for a documentary called *An Inconvenient Truth,* which was turned down by absolutely every movie studio at least twice over a period of two years, and yet somehow had a message that was so important and had such positive energy going for it that it won an Oscar as Best Documentary.

You can see by looking at the lyric that there are three distinct sections to the song, the verse, the chorus, and the bridge. The melody is different in each of the three sections, and so is the lyric. The verses have the same *melody* each time they're sung, but the *words* are different, while the lyric of the chorus is identical each time through. The bridge lyric is completely different from the lyric of the other two sections. It's also important to note that the rhythm of each section is completely different from the rhythm of the other two. *Three sections, three melodies, three rhythms, three lyrics.*

In most songs, the title appears in the chorus, either in the first line or the last line. But since this tune was written for a movie, where the song was used as subtext, Melissa was very clever to slide her title into a verse, rather than hit us over the head by repeating it over and over on what would have been the title line.

Since most of you will not start your careers by writing for Vice President Gore or one of his film projects, I highly recommend that you place your titles strategically in the first or last lines of your choruses. It's important in marketing the song for your audience to be able to figure out what it's called. They're used to assuming that the first or last line of the chorus is the title. So once again, give them what they want.

What impressed me most about this lyric, and all of Melissa's writing, is her passion. Bruce Springsteen once told me that his job as a songwriter was to make his audience care about the things he was passionate about. Using that job description, Melissa has certainly come through with flying colors.

♪ ♪ ♪

I have a Web site, howtobeahitsongwriter.com, where you can listen to "I Need to Wake Up" and follow along in order to see how the rhythm changes from the verse to the chorus, and how dramatic that change is. It's like an explosion, emphasized by the fact that so many of the chorus lines are repetitive, i.e.: "I need to move / I need to wake up / I need to change / I need to shake up / I need to speak out / Something's gotta break up." All that repetition is powerful and potent, especially in a chorus. It worked for Melissa. It will work for you, too.

The title is the lyric half of "the hook." Every hit song needs one. By definition, the hook is the part of the song that draws you in and keeps you listening. *It is the strongest line of the lyric sung on top of the strongest line of melody.* When you find yourself singing in the shower, you're singing the hook. What's even more surprising, you may not have realized that you even liked the song you're singing. If you whistle a tune while you make coffee or wipe the pigeon poop off your garden gate, you're whistling the hook. I've often awakened in the morning with a song running through my head. The part of the song I'm hearing is the hook. I know you've had that experience, too.

Now that you understand what a lyric hook is, be aware that the music has to have hooks, too. Without them, nobody will ever notice or hear your work. Besides being vehicles for us to express ourselves, songs serve as a way to share our feelings with our audience. In order to ensure ourselves of having an audience, we have to hook them.

Beginning songwriters often fall into the trap of making their work too symmetrical. They feel if the first line of a song has eight beats, each of the following lines has to match. Not so. It would make your lyrics much more interesting to have the lines vary in length. Try a verse with lines of three, nine, seven, and two syllables. You'll surprise yourself with how interesting the rhythm will be.

Verses don't have to be just four lines long. They can be five or five and a half or even just three. The only thing I do recommend is they time out to twenty-five seconds, more or less, no matter how many lines you write. Remember, a song is not a novel.

Many new lyricists send me their work for consultation, and while there has been some gorgeous writing crossing my desk, the main problem I keep seeing is the acres of words per song. Sometimes an 8½" × 11" page is completely full of words, and might even have a couple of additional pages, similarly jammed, as the lyric continues. That's too many words. No matter how brilliant, less is more. Try to write each of your lyrics so they fit on one page, and *that* page has lots of white space on it.

If you're writing your lyrics first and are then going to find a composer to write music for them, changing the meter by varying the lengths of the lines will help your musical partner create something that is melodically *unpredictable*. The fewer beats lyrically, the greater chance the composer has to create a memorable melody.

Whenever you listen to songs, try to imagine the lyrics being typed across a page, one line on the page for each line of lyric. If you train yourself to hear a song this way, you can automatically teach yourself to study the structure of every one you hear. It will prove to you how every hit has a simple and basic shape, which is just like a floor plan. The art takes over once that plan is made.

♪ LISTEN TO THE COLORS

In my first songwriting workshop, the instructor underlined each single rhyme ("joke," "Coke") in red, each double rhyme ("jingle," "mingle") in green, each triple rhyme ("banana," "Havana") in blue. He circled all the picture words ("Porsche," "goat") in yellow. Intense feelings were circled in orange. His theory was: the more colorful and illegible the lyrics were after you went through them with your crayons, the better. If you just have a series of red underlines and your song doesn't feel or sound terrific yet, perhaps you need to add color—a picture or a double rhyme. I like to shoot for at least three colors in each song.

Exercise

As an exercise, write a new lyric to the melody of "I Need to Wake Up." You can hear it at howtobeahitsongwriter.com. Choose a subject that is completely different. One of my clients called her song "Groaning Blue Socks." Put your title at the beginning of the chorus no matter where it is in the original song. There are four syllables in the title line, so I want your title to have four syllables as well. Make a list of a hundred silly, meaningless things that have four syllables and put the stresses in the same places as in "I Need to Wake Up." From your list of playful titles, pick one that flows best with Melissa's melody, and remember, *you're just borrowing it for the purpose of this exercise.* As you write, put one syllable of your original lyric where each syllable is in the existing song. Try not to add any beats or your lyric will feel crowded and won't "sing" well. Stay as close to the original form as possible. Remember, you're used to Melissa Etheridge's lyric, so allow yourself some distance and give your own ideas time to develop. Write about whatever feels appropriate to accompany the music. One piece of advice, though: the most lasting and remunerative songs are love songs.

When you have a draft of your new lyric, sing it to the melody of "I Need to Wake Up." Be sure you don't put the emphasis on the wrong syllable. Keep the accents and the language as natural as if you were speaking to someone.

Don't compete with Melissa for greatness. Just do the assignment as best you can. If you're stuck for an idea, try writing something funny. It worked for my client when she wrote "Groaning Blue Socks" and the sequel, "Faxing the Floor." It'll work for you, too, by going for humor instead of fighting to make it count. The demand won't seem as great, so the exercise will be fun. And I feel writing should always be fun.

If you've only got one verse and a chorus, that's okay. If you've only got one line, that's okay, too. If you only have a feeling about what you think the song is saying to you, that's a beginning. The main thing is to

get started and to applaud yourself, giving yourself permission to proceed. It's likely your first songs won't win Oscars, so make peace with
that and be prepared to write your verses and choruses over and over
again, maybe even fifty or a hundred times. That's normal. Songs don't
usually arrive in whole chunks. They often come out a phrase at a time.
Your first lyrics might take a week or a month to finish. But that's
normal. Frustrating but normal.

Most songs on the charts are about love and probably always will be.
But you can take any idea and make it into a love song. If you're
obsessed about a race car, you could structure your lyric so that a love
affair takes place near a racetrack. You can use car analogies in the lyric
and let the music imitate the force, drive, and urgency of the race—
and still have a love song.

I remember my first visit to the British Museum. I'd been studying
literature and assumed Shakespeare, Keats, Shelley, and the guys sat
down at their desks and wrote whole, perfect poetry right off the tops
of their heads. I can't tell you how gratifying it was to see early drafts of
their work in the display cases with words and whole lines crossed out.
It worked for Keats; it'll work for you.

♪ CLICHÉ CONTROL

There is a tendency among all developing writers to use clichés—
phrases we've heard of over and over again in songs but which shouldn't
be there. "I'm on the shelf," "I'm blue," and "morning light" are the
phrases that come immediately to mind and cause the same negative
response in me as fingernails scratching on a blackboard. The true test
of whether a word or phrase should be in a lyric is *not* whether you
can get away with it because somebody famous did, but *if you're saying
something new* and it sounds as natural as a conversation.

Like most writers, I've felt alone in my life, and I've expressed that
isolation in a thousand ways. But I've never *said*, "I'm on the shelf."
That is an expression that was acceptable in the forties and may still be
lurking around, but *only* because it rhymes with "self" and nothing else
does. However, just because a word rhymes is not a good enough
reason to use it. It has to say what you mean. I've never used the phrase
and none of my successful colleagues have, either. Therefore, it doesn't

belong in our songs. If you want to say that you've been by yourself and make it rhyme, try working with "I've been alone" instead. That sounds much more natural and leaves you many more choices for rhymes. So get off your shelves and write in the vernacular.

Like many writers, I'm moody, and whenever I've been unhappy, I've told my friends "I'm depressed," "I'm bummed," "I'm down." But I've never said, "I'm blue." That, too, is a dated cliché. We're writing songs for now, so our lyrics have to sound contemporary. I've heard some wonderful, seductive lines in my time, but no man has ever asked me to stay with him till the "morning light." I've heard, "I want to stay with you all night" or "please don't go home till tomorrow," but I've never heard this "morning light" phrase anywhere except in a bad lyric. Leikin's first law is to sing it the way you say it. If you wouldn't say it, don't sing it, either.

I've included a second song below with a solid verse/chorus, verse/chorus, bridge/chorus structure. You can hear it at howtobeahitsong writer.com.

SOMEWHERE LEFT OF TEXAS
by Molly-Ann Leikin/Bob Algie

I was out of gas, the Triple A was slow
It was raining, I was freezing, you pulled up and smiled let's go
I'm not sure of anything else except I was with you
Never been a person these things happen to (happen to)
We went

CHORUS:
Maybe east, maybe north, maybe south southwest
Hang a U, run a light, ripping 93
Up a hill, cross a bridge, shining in the sun
Somewhere left of (somewhere left of) Texas

All the stars came out, every light was green
Our connection was a blessing with pure hot lightning in between
Just when I was feeling sure that we'd go on and on (and on)
I turned to say I love you, but you had up and gone (up and gone)
You went

CHORUS

BRIDGE:
Maybe I dreamed the whole thing
Maybe I'll never know
But I'll always miss you

CHORUS

© 2008 Red Amaryllis Music.

"Somewhere Left of Texas" is one of my brand-new songs and hasn't been recorded yet. However, it does everything a hit is supposed to do, and I have high hopes for this one.

It tells a story. The lyric is very visual, emotional, and does something we're not supposed to do, but dream of doing anyway, which is running off on an adventure with a stranger. The lyric sets up the story by saying, "I was out of gas, the Auto Club was late, it was raining, I was freezing, and you came along, smiled, and truthfully, I didn't think I had any other choice because I thought I'd die out there on that road. It was scary, romantic, and I sure wasn't the kind of person who had adventures like this." Then the chorus tells us where they went (or was it where they might have gone?) on that adventure. Maybe east, maybe north, maybe south southwest, they hung a U, they ran a light, and they were speeding at ninety-three miles an hour, crossing bridges, roaring up hills and around the bend. And where were they? Somewhere left of Texas.

When I saw that line hiding in another lyric that Bob Algie sent to me for consultation, I went crazy. I've been a songwriter all my life and I have never seen a line as irresistible as that one. It could have been somewhere east of Texas, somewhere north of Texas, but by saying "left," it takes the story into a whole new dimension of fantasy, uncertainty, and romance. Don't most of us live in fear these days of terrorists and stock market instability and losing our jobs, trying to stay current with our credit cards, raising our kids to be good citizens, hoping to God they don't become drug addicts and bounce from one rehab place to another the way so many young people do? As of this writing, we have to be careful with our lives, we can't take chances, or go running off with strangers, because there are too many terrible consequences we hear about all day, every day, on CNN. But human nature is such that we *wish* we could go, chuck everything, drive out to the airport at 150 miles an hour, hop on the first plane out of here, no matter where it's going. Never mind the security, never mind the bag checks, never mind the cost or the consequences. Just get on that plane and go wherever it's going and meet some fabulous stranger on board and have the time of our lives. Most of us are so squashed by fear that we wouldn't dare even verbalize a wish to have that kind of thing happen to us. But it's okay to *sing* about it.

In the second verse of "Somewhere Left of Texas," the story becomes romantic and sensual, very sexy, and then absolutely devastating when the Good Samaritan up and disappears right when the singer thought, "This one is a keeper."

Then in the bridge, she says she isn't sure if she dreamed it or if it was true, but there's part of her that is always going to miss him, no matter what.

The lyric is very, very visual. It is like watching a movie. She was out of gas, so you could see the car pulled over by the side of the road. You know what that is like to sit there, waiting for the Auto Club to show up. And in my mind, the singer was stranded on a very dark stretch of highway. "It was raining, I was freezing." You can *feel* that. And out of the darkness, out of the cold and out of the fear, comes some kind of vehicle, with somebody in it who smiled and said, "Hey, let's go." We didn't say what kind of vehicle it was on purpose, so the listener could supply that information in his imagination and make it very personal.

Some people we read about in newspapers and in magazines and hear about on the news are the kind of folks who hold their noses and jump into all kinds of experiences that most of us are afraid to try. The singer certainly wasn't one of those people. She was just a regular day-to-day lady, trying to live her life, and she figured, "What the heck, I need a ride home."

One of the main purposes of a song, any song, is to give the listener something intense and emotional that is missing from his day-to-day life. A passionate love song like this fulfills the same fantasy that afternoon soap operas do. It offers an escape from an existence that is generally mechanical, humdrum, and routine. I feel "Somewhere Left of Texas" does that.

In my book *How to Be a Hit Songwriter*, there are a lot of additional insider tips on writing great lyrics. You can find that book at howtobeahitsongwriter.com.

2

The Melody

Now that you understand what a lyric hook is, be aware that the music has to have hooks, too. Without them, nobody will ever notice or hear your work. Besides being vehicles for us to express ourselves, songs serve as a way for us to share our feelings with the audience. In order to ensure ourselves of having an audience, we have to hook them.

The lead sheets for "I Need to Wake Up" by Melissa Etheridge, and "Somewhere Left of Texas," which I wrote with Bob Algie, are included in this chapter. If you read music, you will find it helpful in understanding the structure of the tunes. If you don't read music, please go to howtobeahitsongwriter.com, where I've placed the songs so you can hear them.

"I Need to Wake Up" is very well crafted with a classic verse/chorus, verse/chorus, bridge/chorus structure. The melody and rhythm of the verse are completely different from the melody and rhythm of the chorus and the bridge. In the verse, there are two distinct melodic and rhythmic sections. The first starts with "Have I been sleeping" and ends on "distant rumblings." The second starts with "Take me where I am supposed to be" and ends with "to comprehend the things I can't see." Then the chorus comes in with a dramatic change in the melody and the rhythm. The tune goes *up* to the chorus on "I need to *move*," and stays up throughout that whole section. It is also very repetitive, which makes it easy to remember and very sing-alongable. After hearing the first few lines of this chorus, it's impossible not to join in, which is exactly how a chorus melody should be. Then Melissa goes back to the verse melody. The second verse, like the first, has two sections. After that, Melissa repeats her irresistible, sing-alongable chorus, and when it's complete, she blasts into the bridge on "I am not an island," where the rhythm and the melody change again. At the end of the bridge, she sings the chorus one more time, and if we're not singing along with her, we must be deaf. This is what the industry calls a "killer" chorus. If you were to hum or whistle or sing it a cappella in the shower, it would still be terrific, one note at a time, without any instruments.

In constructing a melody, there are several guidelines to follow. Most hit songs are thirty-two bars long. A bar is a popular name for a measure, which is enclosed in vertical lines on the music staff, and indicates a regular, prescribed number of beats. The first measure, or bar, of "I Need to Wake Up" starts with "Have I been sleeping." Some songs have thirty-one bars, some thirty-three, because while they follow the guidelines of form, they aren't stuck in it. Music *is* an art form, after all. But no matter how many bars you have in your song, you should get to the hook within twenty-five seconds. So keep your introductions short—maybe as few as eight bars.

The introduction is the instrumental section that begins the song, which doesn't officially start until the verse melody and the lyric come in. Often writers who are in love with their software go on for as many as sixteen or thirty-two bars of intro before beginning the actual song. Don't. Eight bars are plenty. You've got to hook your audience fast. They'll only give you a few seconds of ear time and then move on to something else that grabs them more easily. Don't go losing them in a long, repetitive intro.

In trying to understand why it's so important to hook an audience quickly, consider commercials and jingles. Their purpose is to sell you a product in twenty seconds. Now they're shortening the length of commercial spots to fifteen seconds, so the message has to be even more compact. The same holds true for melodies. You only get a few seconds to interest your audience in your product. So don't expect anyone to sit patiently waiting for something to happen. *Make* it happen early.

After the title, the melody is the most important part of the song. Lyricists might be upset hearing this, but it is the truth. Make peace with that. The melody is the first thing we hear. If we like it, we'll stay tuned. We respond in a very open, natural, subjective state—like babies.

I know you've seen toddlers dancing and singing to music when you know they don't understand a syllable of the lyric. The toddler test is a really good way to judge the merits of a tune, especially an up-tempo or rhythmic one.

When we hear a melody, we either like it or we don't. If we do, it usually isn't until we've heard it several times that we finally hear the words. You can have a brilliant lyric, but if your song has a weak melody, nobody will ever hear any of it because the melody hasn't done its job. *The function of the melody is to reach out and grab us in an unguarded, primitive, totally emotional state and hold our attention long enough for the more civilized and intellectual lyric to take hold and give us some words to sing.* Don't expect the lyric to do the melody's job.

The music of the verse shouldn't be any longer than twenty-five seconds. Tops. Before a recent seminar I gave for the songwriters in Hollywood, I studied two tunes recorded by Carrie Underwood that were on the Hot 100 *Billboard* chart and found drastic rhythmic and melodic changes occurring in the verses every ten seconds or so. The songs are "Next Time He Cheats" and "Small." That's what you're competing with, so don't dismiss these examples as trivial or accidental. They're not. They're the industry standard, so make sure your melodies are interesting and hooky enough to compete with what you hear on the charts.

Whatever you do melodically, keep your audience *surprised.* If the tune is too predictable, you'll lose everybody. Fast. And once they go, they're gone forever. Remember—you need *magic* in your melodies. You're not just writing music by the pound.

The range of most pop singers is an octave and three—middle C to the E in the octave above it. An octave is eight notes—the musical distance, for example, from middle C to the next C up the scale. If you write a song with a range greater than an octave and three notes, you'll be hard-pressed to find a singer with the ability, or "chops," to handle it. My song "An American Hymn" had a range of an octave and five. I didn't write the melody, but thank God for Placido Domingo, who recorded it. I doubt anybody else could have hit the high notes, and then I would be minus a platinum record. In your writing, don't count on the Domingos to save you. As beautiful as "An American Hymn" is, nobody else ever sang it until Lee Holdridge and I fixed the bridge, so now the range of the song is an octave and three, and "AAH," as we call it, gets recorded once a month.

Most hit "power" ballads, such as Daughtry's "Home," end their verses on lower notes than the ones on which the chorus starts. As a rule, to create tension and drama in a melody, always go up in a chorus, not down. The most effective jump is a major third—C to E, for example. More and more these days, rock songs break the rule of going up, but you can be sure the rhythmic hooks at the beginning of the choruses are strong enough to overcome the melody's drop and keep us listening.

While watching the American Music Awards, I was really impressed by how rhythmic the new crop of hits is on every chart. What particularly got to me was Fergie's song "Big Girls Don't Cry," with that great jolt from the verse to the chorus. One of the strongest pop hooks of the year is in Daughtry's song "Home." I also refer my clients who are looking for great models to study to the work of Rascal Flatts and their song "Take Me There." Listen to Avril Lavigne, One Republic, and Maroon 5, especially "It Won't Be Soon Before Long." I also noticed extraordinary rhythmic changes in the work of Akon, Ne-Yo, and T-Pain.

Listen to Jordin Sparks. And to the Jonas Brothers, the teen idols who sing "S.O.S.," to Taylor Swift and Justin Timberlake, Macon and Timbaland. Listen to "Irreplaceable" by Sugarland, in which there's an irresistible and seductive change in rhythm in the chorus. You will discover that no matter what the genre, whether it's pop, country, rock, rap, hip-hop or R & B, a strategic rhythmic *and* melodic change in the tune is essential to the success of the song and consequently the record.

Most people are more comfortable writing lyrics than music, because we speak words and we write words. We use them all the time, so we practice daily. But we don't speak music. That's okay. Music is something we *feel*, something we hear inside our heads and in our hearts. And we feel all the time. So don't be intimidated by your clumsy musicianship or your inability to read music or even play an instrument. Many of the world's greatest musicians never write original songs; they just interpret what other people have already written. Don't feel you have to be a great keyboard player or guitarist to write a strong melody. Having some musical "chops" would certainly help you create melodies, but it isn't mandatory. If you hear a tune inside your head, you can whistle it into a recording device and then hire an arranger to embellish it with chords. *The melody is just a series of single notes you can hum or sing in the shower.* There aren't necessarily any chords or arrangements involved in its conception.

When I write a song, I always write the melody first, one note at a time. While I have limited chops as a keyboard player, I do hear contagious, irresistible melodies in my head. I keep a recording device of some kind with me all the time, in my car, in my purse, next to the bed, even in the shower, so that whenever I get an idea for something, I just sing it into the recording device, whether it's an old cassette machine or an MP3 player. Sometimes I even call my voice mail and sing to myself. I constantly revise the notes, going over and over and over them. You may work differently, but just remember that songwriting is a process, and usually what comes out in the first draft is just that—a first draft—and usually needs several more to reach the finish line. I'm lucky in that I feel a little click in my gut when I know something I've written is finished. But I don't have anything to do with chords or programming until much later.

I record the single notes of the chorus and then I work backwards to write the individual notes of the verse, one note at a time. When I am finally happy with both the verse and the chorus, I go looking for the chords to put around them. That way, I'm not inhibited by my lack of musicianship or intimidated by the technical aspects of programming. I just write the song. Once the melody's down pat and the lyric I write to the melody clicks and I have the chords that go around the notes, then I start thinking about "how do I hear this produced, what instruments do I feel, what record on the radio sounds like what I'm going for?" *But it all starts with the individual notes of the melody.* I know from working with so many talented developing writers that they start with too much ambition and too much technology and not enough bare simple note-by-note creativity. So if you find your melodies aren't as strong as you would like them to be, or that the marketplace requires, then I suggest you try some version of my way of writing songs and adapt it to your personality. When you change the process, you can change the result.

For most songwriters, writing music is not a matter of deciding about quarter notes and staccato sixteenths and minor thirds. It is simply a process of turning their feelings into music. If you feel something deeply and it causes you to stop in the middle of the day and race to the piano or pick up the guitar, that's writing. I suggest you keep some kind of recording device running at all times when you compose, so you don't have to worry about remembering what you just heard. You say you'll remember, but you won't.

When new clients come to me, they often have weak, predictable melodies and ask me to suggest chord progressions that will make their music more interesting. The truth is no chord pattern can strengthen a weak tune. If a composer has gotten into a hole melodically, it's because he is not writing *pure* melody. He's relying on the chords to create the tune for him. Write the simple melodic line first and *then* go find the chords that enhance it.

Contrary to whatever you've seen romanticized and fantasized in movies, most contemporary writers do not "write" their songs on staff paper while the songs are being created. Composers get their melodies down on a recording device and then either write out the melody on staff paper later or use Sibelius software to do it for them.

Once you have a melody line that you like, one that's catchy and doesn't sound like anything else you've heard, decide which part of the song it is. See what goes with it, just as if you were coordinating your wardrobe. You wouldn't use two shades of red that clash. Be sure your music doesn't, either.

If you've got the first line of the chorus, finish the melody to the whole chorus and then work backwards to create a verse melody that leads up to the first line of the chorus. It's always helpful to write the chorus melody first, just as with the lyric, because everything has to relate to it. Otherwise, you're just writing blind. If the line of the melody you've written feels like a verse, then you know you should be building on that line musically and emotionally to lead up to the chorus. Usually the highest note of the song is in that section.

Just as each lyrical phrase should relate to the title, every musical phrase should also relate to the music of the title line. It should all belong in the same song. The famous four notes of Beethoven's Fifth wouldn't blend well or belong in the same verse as the title line of "I'm Dreaming of a White Christmas," right? And the chorus of "Blob" wouldn't go with "The Star Spangled Banner." So make sure the feeling and the texture of the music is consistent but interesting and full of surprises at the same time.

For those of you who aren't schooled musicians and don't think of music in technical terms, I suggest you think of it in terms of color. The verses should be lighter shades than the chorus. If you have a mint green verse, the chorus should be emerald. Starting with the first note of the song, the music should gradually build up to the brighter, stronger color of the chorus, using every shade and tint along the way. Pink verse, red chorus.

♪ THE BRIDGE

The bridge is a musical and lyrical section that is only played once, usually right after the verse and chorus have been repeated twice. The melody, lyric, and rhythm of the bridge should be completely different from the verse and the chorus. Look at "Somewhere Left of Texas," which comes later in this chapter, and see how the bridge comes in with a lot of rhythmic punch. It isn't expected and gives the song a big lift after the verse and chorus have been repeated twice each. The bridge hasn't been heard before in the song and surprises us. See, there's that word again. *Surprise.* A bridge simply connects the middle and the end of the song by adding something new to a tune that we think is just going to repeat itself.

I should tell you that I have never met a songwriter—no matter how successful he is—who enjoys or feels inspired when it comes to writing bridges. One of my very talented clients in Japan agonizes over every single bridge he writes, and he's very prolific. I know when I talk to him each Friday afternoon, he is hoping that just this one time he can get away without a third section to his tune. He always writes one even- tually, and it's usually terrific, but he never looks forward to it. A col- league of mine, who was vice president of music at a major studio, sums up bridge work this way: "When I die, if, by some miracle I get into heaven, it will be on the condition that God wants me to rewrite the bridge."

That section can go up or down melodically in the beginning, but in power ballads it usually goes soaring upward at the end into the last, dramatic chorus. One of the best examples of an effective bridge is in

"Taking Chances," written by Linda Perry and sung by Celine Dion. The rhythm changes like a whomp over the head at the beginning of the bridge, where it says, "And I had my heart beaten down / But I always came back for more, yeah," but the real surprise in this bridge is that there is a *second* hook in the middle of it in the section that starts with "So talk to me, talk to me like lovers do." Having two hooks in a bridge has raised the bar for the entire industry, no matter what the genre of the song. Good for you, Linda Perry.

As an ongoing exercise to strengthen your melodic skills, play your favorite songs all the way through on your instrument or sing them a cappella and see how the musical sections change. If you don't play an instrument, listen to the way the colors of the music change and intensify, softening in the verses and building back up to the chorus. Feel those changes and incorporate them into your writing style. Your songs should have those same dramatic, unexpected jolts, too.

With so much music being created these days, and with such great access in our workplaces, homes, cars, dental offices, and rehab facilities, it's easy to "borrow" someone else's melody without even realizing it. One of your responsibilities as a composer is to be thoroughly knowledgeable about every song on every CD, MP3, or that's available for download. It sounds like an overwhelming task, I know, but it's your job to be aware of what other people in your field have already done so you don't duplicate or infringe on their work. If you were a scientist who wanted to invent something, wouldn't you check around carefully first to be sure you weren't duplicating someone else's effort? I know I would. I'd hate for you to think you'd written a hit, have you make an expensive demo, get it to the number-one group that's about to release it, and *then* find yourself slapped with a major lawsuit that could wipe you out forever. Know the literature and commerce of your craft. Be aware of everything that's come before you. Then when you write a melody, you can be sure it's yours and yours alone.

Exercise

Write a melody to the lyric of "I Need to Wake Up." You have a well-structured lyric to use as your guide. Put one note of music on each syllable of the lyric. Make sure as you sing the new song that you stress the words as you would when speaking them. Don't put the em*pha*sis on the wrong syl*la*ble. You can change the rhythm of the verses to 3/4 (waltz time), 5/8, 2/2, 7/11, or whatever you like. Nothing has to be the same as it is in the original melody except the form—ABAB. You can write a bridge if you want to, but for your first few songs, it isn't mandatory. Make sure that your melody goes *up* in the chorus. I recommend a jump of a major third.

Remember—*a hit melody is a series of single notes joined together in a memorable but unexpected pattern.* It's not a bunch of gnarly sounds or rhythm riffs you found in your synthesizer. That's a track, not a tune. A melody is what you sing *over* the track. It's what you whistle, what you hum, what you play with one finger on the piano. A good test of whether a tune will be a hit or miss is if you can play it in seven notes or less and recognize it like they did on *Name That Tune.* If you think you can fill in the holes with background vocals or slick riffs, or "fix it in the studio," you're really acknowledging the melody's weaknesses and inability to stand up on its own.

Because of software like Pro Tools, it's easy for composers to fall into what I call the "technical toy trap." That's when they start to rely on their instruments or machines to do their composing for them. In order to avoid this pitfall, try to hear the melody in your head first. Don't just play or strum chords and wait for the notes to fall in between and bounce out at you. *Hear* the music in your head. Once you write the simple melody line of the tune, then, of course, go to your instrument to embellish it. But don't rely on software to do your initial creating for you. Trust your gut and your heart to tell you what you're feeling and what needs to be translated into music.

Many of my new clients who play guitar often write weak melodies. The guitar is a great rhythm instrument, absolutely, but since most guitarists don't pick out individual notes, they simply play chords. I've urged thousands of songwriters to switch to keyboards when creating their melodies, and write note by note. Then when the tune is finished, I suggest they go back to their guitars and add the chords. They are usually happily surprised with the results, which are more tuneful tunes, not just predictable chord progressions.

Many clients who don't write lyrics tell me that they only write "instrumentals" and simply don't deal with words. Some cite the success of the one, lonely instrumental per year that makes it into the charts.

A few composers go so far as to tell me their melodies don't need words. But I point out to them that since absolutely every vocalist and group needs whole songs with lyrics to sing, they have the very least chance for success if they write instrumentals only. I suggest to writers who insist their music doesn't need words that they make a deal with their egos: for every instrumental piece they write for themselves, write one song with words and music for the marketplace. That way they allow themselves to continue doing what they love best, but they also greatly increase their chances of success by writing complete songs.

For more insider tips on structuring great melodies, I recommend you read my book *How to Be a Hit Songwriter*, available at howtobeahit songwriter.com.

♪ JOINT WORK

If you write lyrics only or tunes only, you should know that once a lyric is added to a preexisting melody, it becomes joint work. Even if that piece of music is played instrumentally thereafter, the lyricist is considered a co-author and is half owner of the copyright. When you collaborate, make sure you get everything in writing and never assume you can trust anybody you're working with, especially a friend or relative. In this business, relationships without written documentation go south very quickly, especially when there is a lot of money at stake.

♪ ♪ ♪

Enjoy your creative process. Writing is supposed to be fun. Don't push yourself too hard. Creating takes time. Give it to yourself. It may take a day, a week, or a month. That's fine, because when something beautiful or catchy is finished, all we remember is the song, not the struggle that went into creating it. I'd rather have a half-finished tune that sparkles and promises to be special than a dozen completed songs that are iffy at best, sounding like everything else I've already heard.

By now, you've written a brand-new ABAB lyric that is well structured. And you've written a brand-new melody to that wonderful lyric of yours. Congratulations! You've just written what could be your first hit!

The more you write, the better you get. The more your write, the easier it is to write. And the more you write, the better your chances are for each new song being your first million seller. Now let's study the structure of another well-crafted song.

The lead sheet for "Somewhere Left of Texas" is included in this chapter. For those of you who don't read music, you can find the song at howtobeahitsongwriter.com. You will notice that the verse melody is very simple and easy to remember but not predictable. Each of the lines of the verse melody is different. I did that on purpose so the tune wouldn't sound too obvious and the audience wouldn't know what was coming. The trick is to make them think they know what's ahead and surprise them. The rhythm in the chorus is dramatically different from the rhythm in the verse, and the melody in the chorus is very repetitive and, consequently, easy to remember. This is a good example of how a chorus can often sound like a nursery rhyme for adults. The more sing-alongable and repetitive, the better. And the surprise jolt at the beginning of the last line of the chorus creates another hook. So you can see how the melody and the rhythm work together.

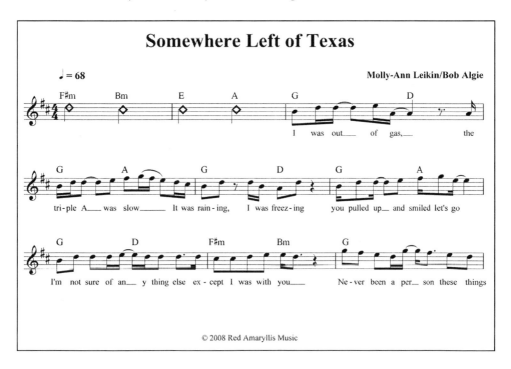

Exercise

Write a new melody for "Somewhere Left of Texas," substituting one new note for each syllable of lyric in the original song. Try not to add any extra ones. In your version, I want you to put your title in the first line of the chorus, not in the last, which will make it much easier. You might have to remove yourself from the song for a few days to get the old melody out of your head. *Please note: You can't keep our melody or our lyric. This is only an exercise. Thank you for respecting our copyright.*

When you get the tune finished, you'll have completed your second well-structured commercial song. That's a cause for celebration! I'm very proud of you! I want you to be, too.

Now write a new melody for "I Need to Wake Up," following the same guidelines you used for "Somewhere Left of Texas."

I Need to Wake Up

Words and Music by Melissa Ethridge

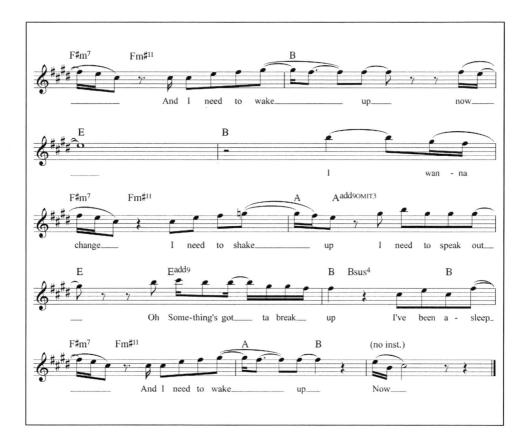

Your next assignment is to do something terrific for yourself as a reward for all of your hard work. This could be the most important step in the creative process. I like to buy myself flowers. Perhaps for you it's ice cream, theater tickets, or a new sweater. You might want to take a drive in the country. Whatever you do, make a point of acknowledging that you're doing it as a reward for what you've just created. It is a victory in itself, just because you did it—not because your song sold a million copies or was downloaded sixty times a second on iTunes. The victory starts with you.

One of my most determined clients has made great strides in her writing in just two sessions with me. But she seems to have reached a plateau, and I'm convinced it's because she can't tell herself she's done a good job. At least she is aware of the problem. And we're working on it.

This is a hurdle many songwriters have to overcome. Though they're thrilled with their writing and with the new approaches they learn, there is a part of their creative ego that is terribly frustrated and demands success immediately. Don't let past attempts and failures get in your way. The songs you wrote two or twenty years ago that missed have absolutely nothing to do with what you are doing now. As far as I'm concerned, they don't exist. It isn't fair to contaminate your new work with the unfulfilled dreams and demands of your old material.

So be fair to yourself. Never mind if you've been writing for years and haven't gotten anyplace yet. By the time you finish this book, you'll have a lot of valuable information you never had before, or to which you were never receptive. You'll be a better writer just for taking the initiative to find out what you *should* be doing that you're *not* doing. That is a tremendous step.

If you reward yourself sufficiently, your creative ego will be happy to accommodate you the next time you set out to write your feelings down on paper. It will be a little easier because you've already done it and acknowledged it with something immediate and tangible. Be sure you reward yourself for everything you write—a phrase, a title, a little swatch of melody. It'll help keep your creativity flowing.

Exercise

I suggest you listen to ten current hit songs that you love to see how the choruses repeat, how they go up or down, and especially how the rhythm changes when the chorus begins. Then make a deal with yourself to study one new song each day for a month. Choose some Web sites and stations you don't normally listen to. In fact, one of the first assignments I give my new clients is to change all the buttons on their car radios and delete all the favorite Web sites they have marked on their computers. Make that your assignment, too. Meanwhile, you'll be learning the intrinsic value of structure in songwriting.

For more insider tips on writing strong melodies, I recommend you read *How to Be a Hit Songwriter*, available at howtobeahitsongwriter.com.

3

Rhyming

Great songs have to say something. They are feelings, situations, and stories set to music. Rhyming makes them accessible and memorable. Children are drawn to nursery rhymes and remember them easily because the repetitive sounds and rhythms stay with them. There is a child in the personality of every adult. So adults can also be reached easily through rhyme and repetition. You could say that the simplest songs on the radio are really adult nursery rhymes.

You may ask yourself why you should lose sleep trying to make things rhyme and say something unique when all you hear are bad lyrics and bad rhymes on the air anyway. I'll answer by saying you've chosen the wrong examples: There are many songs on the radio that *do* say something extraordinary in a passionate way and rhyme at the same time. And these are the songs that tend to become big hits and continue to be played year after year.

What is a rhyme? A perfect one is "day," "way," "hay," "gray." An imperfect one is "day," "way*s*," "gray*ed*." While I always strive for perfect rhymes in my own work and often drive my collaborators up the wall with my meticulousness, I think my songs are better as a result. It took me a long time before I could accept a near or "bastard" rhyme in a song. Rhyming can make a good song better. But obviously it's more important to write lyrics that mean something and say something in a new, imaginative way than merely to make the words rhyme.

All good lyricists feel they should go for the perfect rhyme over the imperfect one, but that it's better to say something scintillating that doesn't rhyme than just say something ordinary that does. My guess is that if Oscar Hammerstein II came down from rock and roll heaven today and tuned in to a pop station, he'd be horrified by all the sloppy rhymes. But at the same time he'd probably be intrigued with the new vocabulary writers are using, all the new ways of conveying feelings, ideas, and emotions.

I shoot for perfect rhymes. As an artist I shouldn't impose my values on you. I will only say that lyric writing is a craft and rhyming is part of that craft. On the other hand, any good lyricist will also say it's more important to write something original than to make things rhyme for the sake of rhyming. The song "Live Like You Were Dying," which was a huge hit for Tim McGraw and number one for ten weeks, uses some unusual rhymes—some perfect, some not. They include "X-rays and next days," which to my knowledge, have never appeared in a hit pop country song before. So good for Tim Nichols and Craig Wiseman for reaching and stretching and going for something new. Any good lyricist would forgive an imperfect rhyme in favor of a great story and an intensely emotional situation like this one, in which the singer met someone who was diagnosed with cancer and was told by his doctor to live every day to the very, very fullest. With that advice, he went skydiving, climbed the Rocky Mountains, rode a bull, loved more completely, was nicer to people, forgave them, and made absolutely every second count, which is something we should all do anyway, isn't it? He became a better husband, a better friend, he made time to go fishing, and he even read the Bible.

Another song I love and really admire is called "Next Time He Cheats," which was a monstrous hit for Carrie Underwood and number one for five weeks. The song's writers, Chris Tompkins and Josh Kear, used a lot of near rhymes, but they also include some fabulous pictures, making this song and its story of heartbreak and retribution just like a movie. Because the lyrics are so original and passionate, we forgive the slant rhymes. When the singer finds out her boyfriend has been cheating on her with a bleach-blond tramp, she carves her name into his leather seats, takes a baseball bat, a Louisville Slugger to be exact, to both headlights, and slashes all of his tires. (There's a woman after my own heart!) I'm not suggesting you all run out and wreck your exes' cars. But because this song is so passionate and visual, we overlook the near rhyme and see ourselves vicariously getting even. The fantasy makes it fun to listen to, and is as gratifying as the last scene in the movie *Crash*, where the nasty HMO clerk gets rear-ended on Christmas Eve.

Most writers make their songs rhyme at the end of the line. People expect rhymes there, but in an attempt to surprise and entertain the listener you might try moving the rhymes around. Instead of writing, "I wish there were a boy for me, tall and cute as he can be," you might try, "I wish there were a boy for me, and he'd be cute and extr*emely* tall." The "e" sound carries throughout the line and makes an internal rhyme connecting the lyric in places we don't expect. It also jogs the rhythm. Remember, your job is to surprise the audience. Don't give them what they're expecting or they'll change stations on you.

There are some rhymes I stay away from simply because they are so predictable. When you use "double," you know "trouble" and "bubble" are nearby. However, if you precede them with an unexpected adjective, your audience will be surprised. "Sweet trouble" or "Half a double" are good examples of this.

You will notice that many words that we use in our daily vocabulary don't sing. "Garbage disposal knob" isn't particularly mellifluous. Neither is "bank vault" or "hard disk." The words that are generally considered most singable—"love," "heart," "need," "want," "miss," "long," "touch," and "hold"—have been used to death. Your job as a lyricist is to find a new singing vocabulary for your songs. "Orange" doesn't rhyme with anything, but it does sing. So instead of using a near rhyme, use the "or" sound in the next line a couple of times to carry out the rhyme. "I gave him m*ore or*anges. He n*or*mally *or*dered m*ore* pears." This way, you're able to use a word that sings, has color, is a picture, isn't used very much, and which, in fact, probably has been avoided because it doesn't rhyme perfectly with anything.

I have a rhyming dictionary. I also have a thesaurus. I got both of them as bat mitzvah gifts. At the time I thought they were boring presents. I obviously wasn't thinking like a songwriter. Now I never sit down to work without both tattered volumes at my side. I may not open either during the writing of a particular lyric, but I have them there for support just in case.

Some people claim that referring to a rhyming dictionary is "cheating." I couldn't disagree more. What the rhyming dictionary gives is a long list of possible rhyme sounds that will either provide you with the word you need or steer you in the right direction. No matter how many hours I spend at my desk, it's usually when I'm away from my writing—taking a walk or doing my ever-popular vacuuming—that the word I *do* want pops into my head.

If you use a rhyming dictionary, be careful you're not just rhyming to rhyme. Be sure you're saying what you mean. And be sure it sounds natural—like conversation. That is where the craft of lyric writing comes in.

No matter what your position on rhyming is, lyrics are dialogue for singers. I suggest to my clients, as I suggest to you, that as you write the words, ask yourself three important questions:

1. Have I heard this before?
2. If so, could I make it a little different?
3. If not, could I write something else?

By answering these questions truthfully, you will raise the level of your lyric writing, as well as your chances for success in the marketplace.

4

The All-Important Title

The title of the song is crucial to its success. Given the choice of listening to a tune called "I Want You" and another entitled "Peppermint Tires," I'd take the second. So would any music publisher. And so would most program directors—the people who determine the playlists on all broadcast outlets. Collectively, they listen to thousands of songs each week. The best shot you have at hooking their interest and making them *listen* to your hard work is by using a provocative, fresh title.

The title of a song is just as important as the title of a movie or book. Titles that have appeared recently on the Hot 100 include "Bubbly" by Colbie Caillat, "Paralyzer" by Finger Eleven, "Clumsy" by Fergie, "Tattoo" by Jordin Sparks, "Like You'll Never See Me Again" by Alicia Keys, "Duffle Bag Boy" by Playaz Circle Featuring Lil Wayne, "I'm So Hood" by DJ Khaled Featuring T-Pain, Trick Daddy, Rick Ross, and Plies, and "Shawty Is a 10" by The-Dream. Every one of these titles is intriguing and interesting, and the songs they name deserve to be hits.

Some of the current pop country songs with great titles include "Like Red on a Rose" (my all-time favorite) by Alan Jackson. We're used to hearing "As Red As a Rose" or "A Red Rose for You" or "A Dozen Red Roses," but Jackson has juxtaposed the words to make them catch our eye, our hearts, and bottom line—our ears. I like "The Road and the Radio" by Kenny Chesney and especially appreciate the alliteration. We all feel the connection that the singer has to his radio while he's traveling, because don't we all feel that the music we choose to hear while driving alone is our trusted, treasured, and loving companion? Miranda Lambert's "Crazy Ex-Girlfriend" suggests to me immediately that there is some friction here that is probably funny, and I really want to hear about it so I don't feel as badly about being nuts after I break up with somebody. George Strait's "How 'Bout Them Cowgirls" is positive and supportive of women in general, and cowgirls in particular. It also suggests a romantic theme, which it turns out to be. And I really admire the conflict in the title "Between Raising Hell and Amazing Grace" by Big & Rich. Conflict usually works. That's good writing. And good business, too.

The title of a movie is almost as important as its stars and director. The films in today's newspaper include *Starting Out in the Evening, I Am Legend, The Golden Compass, Enchanted, No Country for Old Men, Hitman, Margot at the Wedding, I'm Not There, Atonement, August Rush, American Gangster,* and *Into the Wild.* Each of these titles has a solid "Gee, I'd really like to see that" factor, which makes us feel excited and right about spending all that money on a movie ticket, a babysitter, parking, popcorn, a drink, a twenty-two-dollar mini-box of Junior Mints, plus the massage therapist you need after being trapped in a bad seat in the theater for almost three hours.

On this week's *New York Times* bestseller list for fiction, the titles include *Playing for Pizza* by John Grisham. What makes this book sound interesting is that the words "playing" and "pizza" are rarely used together, and the juxtaposition makes this title intriguing. Jan Karon's *Home to Holly Springs,* which is alliterative with the *H*'s, also feels somewhat warm and fuzzy, which most of us have a hard time feeling in these days of terrorism and assassination. *The Almost Moon* is a great title because again we are not used to seeing "almost" and "moon" used together. Good for you, Alice Sebold. Same thing in *Tree of Smoke* by Denis Johnson and *The Yiddish Policeman's Union* by Michael Chabon. We're used to hearing about police and unions, but *Yiddish* police? All of these are great titles, each calculated to sell the hardcover book to which it belongs.

A writer can get lucky with a song called "You" or "You and Me" or "Us" or "Ooo Ooo Baby," but if you write lyrics only and you don't sing, I suggest you make sure your contribution to the song and the record is spectacular. The way I look at it is, my name is going on my work. That's my fingerprint. I'm proud of what I do. People who listen to songs know the difference between something that's okay and something that's brilliant. So dig a little deeper and find the part of yourself that's unique and looking to be expressed in a way that no one else has done before. You'll be glad you did.

Some of you will argue with me, claiming that anything with a popular writer's name on it will sell. You're correct, up to a point. But most good writers who are making a living from their writing are smart about marketing. It may not be what you want to hear, but it's true. Songs have to be accessible to the public. People need a headline before they'll commit to buying a newspaper or a magazine. The title is the headline. Give it to them.

No record company wants to risk its investment in a hit artist on a boring title. Their business is to sell records—not to promote esoteric art. To sell records, they need hit titles that'll make the audience respond immediately.

I had one client who wrote lovely melodies but boring titles. As an exercise, I had him go through the brand names of all the cleaning substances under his kitchen sink and see how many song ideas he came up with. For example, "Formula 409" could be the number of the motel room in which a couple is trysting. Or it could be an area code to which a phone call—secret or otherwise—is being made. I bet you never thought of that before. Once when the Santa Ana winds were blowing in from the desert and making my lips very dry, I bought something called Lip Therapy to keep them from chapping. I realized that the name of that tube of moisturizer would make a great title for a song.

Exercise

Go through the shelves under your sink, look in your medicine cabinet, and search your laundry room. See how many brand names you can find that'll work as double entendres. Start with "Vanish" and "Black Flag." My guess is each of you will uncover at least eight more.

Take a title expedition. Go to a store in which you don't ever shop. Look at the brand names and see how creative you can be with them as titles. Maybe "Brooks Brothers" is a song about a girl in love with twins and can't decide which one she wants to marry.

Great titles often come from putting words together that normally don't go together. "Beautiful Sadness," one of the very special songs I wrote with Lee Holdrige, is that kind of title. You can stumble on happy accidents like that while playing the dictionary game, which is described in chapter 7. You'll be surprised how exhilarating it is to discover potential titles from unexpected sources. You'll also be surprised at how much fun you can have in the process. And remember, writing should be fun.

You can't protect a title with a copyright. Technically that means you can use the title of someone else's old song for one of your new ones. But it's bad form. If I discover a title has already been used, I'll discard it or add some words in parentheses to differentiate it from preexisting songs with the same name.

While you can't copyright a title, I think you'd be foolish to write another song called "The Long and Winding Road" or "When Doves Cry" or "I Write the Songs." Even if a publisher likes the song, when he takes it to an artist or a producer, they'll think it's the *old* song and probably won't bother listening to it. So be smart about naming your material. You're unique both as a person and as a writer. Make sure your songs reflect that.

When I started writing, my song titles were so long they wouldn't fit on a record label. They should be short and punchy. Remember my song "In My Dreams I Was Never in Omaha"? Neither does anyone else. How about the ever-popular "Take Your Suitcase Out of My Life"?

Were I writing the first song now, I'd simply call it "Omaha." I'd call the second "Suitcase." When I was a beginner, if I had written "Guilty," the tune Barbra Streisand and Barry Gibb recorded (and which Gibb co-wrote), I probably would've called it "We've Got Nothin' to Be Guilty Of." Just plain "Guilty" has much more snap and punch. Again, less is more. That's something I had to learn and something you'll know instinctively with time.

When searching for a title, one trick I often use is to take a common phrase that has "life" in it and substitute the word "love." Take the phrase, "For the life of me I couldn't think of his name." Now change that to "for the *love* of me" and you've got yourself a hit title. There's a song I recently heard called "I've Got to Learn to Love Without You." See what I mean? Any title that starts you thinking you're going to hear one thing and then presents you with something else serves a double purpose. It tricks you. The audience needs that. In fact, they demand it. One of my earlier efforts was a song written with Steve Dorff called "You Set My Dreams to Music." Most people expected "You Set My *Words* to Music." But using the word "dreams" instead gave this song title some magic and a heightened sense of romance. And it was recorded twenty-five times in eighteen months.

Titles that rhyme internally are especially powerful. My first hit was ''Silver *Wings* and Golden *Rings*.'' (My publisher called it "Silver Things and Onion Rings.") The title works on three levels. First, there are colors in it—silver and gold. It also contains pictures—airplane wings and wedding bands. Finally, it suggests that someone is flying away and someone else is unhappy about it. This third level—conflict—is the key to any successful drama. That tug of war makes for great songs. Think of "Separate Lives" and "Against All Odds." The more star-crossed the lovers in your songs, the better.

Don't ask me where the title "Silver Wings and Golden Rings" came from. I know I wasn't smart enough in those days to sit down at my desk and invent it. It was truly a matter of inspiration. But I quickly realized how good the title was when it passed the "Snuff Garrett test." Snuff was producing hit after hit at the time and had just had a monster record with "Gypsies, Tramps and Thieves." (How's that for a title! See all the pictures it evokes in only four words?) Snuff was famous for only listening to songs with visual titles. Give him a song called "I Miss You" and he'd leave the room. But if he liked your title, he'd dance on his desk and give you the cash to buy an American car.

When a *real* song person hears a title that sizzles, all hell breaks loose. Doors that used to seem welded shut swing wide open. People in pink sunglasses start taking you to lunch in restaurants with no prices on the menus. They send you cases of wine for Christmas that you could trade for a new Porsche. Your lawyer takes your phone calls and journalists learn the correct spelling of your surname. Great titles open big doors. Of course, once you get through them, make sure your songs live up to their names.

5

Collaborating

When you listen to a song, it should sound like a seamless work—whether it's written by one person or five. It should *not* sound like one person's words set to someone else's music. It is one expression. The two components of the song—the words and the music—should feel fused and completely integrated. The process of getting a song to that level requires an understanding of the collaborative process.

The lyricist's job is to translate the feelings of the music into words. The words have to "sing." They have to flow easily and comfortably with the melody. A good contemporary lyric is often the equivalent of dialogue in a conversation. Eavesdrop. Write down what people say. The chances are good you'll be able to borrow some lines of conversation for your lyrics. I had one client who was trying to be original by using the word "imbue" to rhyme with "you." It did follow my first rule, which is to find vocabulary that hasn't been used to death. But it broke the conversational rule—it didn't sound natural.

Be careful not to em*pha*size the wrong syl*la*ble in order to accommodate the music. If you find you're doing that, rewrite the lyric. Maybe the composer can restructure his phrase so the stresses are all natural and conversational. Be aware, however, that English is commonly spoken in iambic pentameter, a metrical pattern in which there are five stressed syllables in a line. An example of this is: "The *boy* on the *bike* rode a*head* of the *truck* on the *street*."

Music, on the other hand, can have any meter. If you write lyrics with long lines of iambic pentameter, you have to give the composer freedom to take words and phrases out here and there to make the melody and its rhythm interesting. At the same time, if you have a million-dollar title, the composer should try to accommodate it. That could simply mean placing it somewhere you didn't expect him to put it.

The bottom line in any successful collaboration is flexibility. Do what's best for the song. Don't be married to a lyric or a melody no matter how long you've walked around with it in your head or on an MP3 before you met your partner. You *have* to accommodate one another. Bending a little here and there is far better than carting around an armful of orphan lyrics or melodies. If you're working in a collaboration, you and your partner need each other.

I want my audience to have a new experience when they hear my lyrics. But I have to be careful about being too wordy. Nobody hums a lyric. They hum melodies. That's the part of the song that first draws in the audience. It *must* prevail. If the audience likes the feel and sound of the music, then and only then will the words be heard. That may be hard for lyricists to accept at first, but it's a reality. Of course a great melody needs a strong lyric as well. But the melody draws people in initially—the lyric keeps them there.

There are three general kinds of songwriting collaborations. In the first, you work alone writing the music and lyrics. The collaboration is between your creative ego and the critic in your head. You are alone, creating and rewriting until you think your song is finished. When it is, you may feel a rush of excitement, unable to wait to play it for somebody. At four in the morning you call a friend in Iowa and scream, "Listen to this!" You play the song. Your sleepy friend says it's a smash—and you're home.

On the other hand, your friend might say he likes the lyric but doesn't like the chorus melody. Or he might love the melody but feels the lyric isn't as strong. You might argue that the song will sound better once you record it properly in a good studio. You could get defensive and say your friend's too tired or too thick to understand it. But as a professional writer, if you get a few negative comments, put the song away for a few days, divert your attention to other things, and then come back to it later with fresh eyes and ears. Distance will allow you some objectivity. You might find that what your friends have said has some validity. And you might have some new ideas of your own. Objectivity is the key here.

Nobody in the heat of creation can step outside his or her song and be anything but subjective. With time, you will hopefully be able to see what your song needs to get it over the top and onto the hit list.

When you write your songs alone, you have to satisfy the creator and the critic within you. Of course, the critic is never satisfied. But we'll deal with him in chapter 6.

Now suppose you're a lyricist. You've been looking for a composer/collaborator for months—even years. You have a stack of good lyrics, and nobody has ever written a melody to any of them that has satisfied you. Maybe there's one lyric you've written that absolutely sizzles. Everybody says it's a hit, but you just don't have the melody yet. You've tried to write it yourself, but you simply haven't got melodies in you right now.

Then along comes a composer with some pomp and dazzle, who sits down at your old upright, plays like Elton John, sings like Carrie Underwood, and you think you've found your other half at last. Often, though, this "discovery" can become a major disappointment. The usual reason is that lyricists get too impatient. They're frustrated seeing their lyrics on paper. They want to *hear* them. But songs aren't complete without music, and while the lyricist may hold out long and hard for the right melody, there comes a time when even the best of them throws in the towel, duped by impatience into feeling he or she has found the perfect tune.

But there is a trick to telling whether or not the melody is a hit. Listen to your collaborator's tune apart from the lyric. Ask yourself if that melody would have inspired you to write your lyric to it. If the answer is yes, you've got a match. If not, you have to go back to the composer. Be diplomatic and encouraging and tell him you feel the melody has some wonderful parts. However, you want every bar to be as good as the best ones he's already written. So you'd like him to think about an alternative to the section or sections that don't quite soar for you yet. If you approach your collaborator in a nurturing and supportive way, he or she will be encouraged to keep at it. If you sound accusing or frustrated, you could close down your partner's creativity, thereby disintegrating your collaboration.

The important thing to remember in any song collaboration is that the completed song is king. A great song is your desired goal. Your aim should be to make the song better. If you feel you're right about one section and your collaborator argues that he's right about the same section and neither of you can bully the other into submission, then the smart thing to do is for both of you to put your favorite versions aside and come up with a third one together. This is what I call finding the compromise candidate. It has worked in every successful collaboration in history and will work for you, too.

Nobody's always right. Collaborating is not a contest. Nobody should win, except the song. When it wins, everybody does. When in doubt, do what's best for the song.

If you're a composer and someone has written a lyric to one of your preexisting melodies, test that lyric by asking yourself if the lyric would have inspired you to write that melody to it. If you get a yes, fine—it's a keeper. But if you find the answer is no, be as diplomatic as possible. Suggest that this is a good beginning, and try to encourage the lyricist to dig a little deeper. Tell your partner you know he or she can come up with great lines because you've seen them in other work. Anyone who's done it once can do it again. You're expecting great things. That's why you wanted to work with this writer in the first place. It's all positive reinforcement.

Above all else, be diplomatic. Often a careless, offhand remark can so undermine a writer's confidence that he or she is afraid to write anymore. It's a good idea to understand your partner's sensitivities and creative process. It's necessary to be as understanding of your partner as you'd like your partner to be of you.

Sometimes your collaborator will need pampering. Occasionally you might have to tell your partner something is great when it isn't just to keep him or her creating. Later, when he or she is feeling more confident, you can say you've been thinking about the song you wrote last week, wondering if there isn't a better way you can both approach the chorus . . .

A major stumbling block for collaborators is possessiveness. Sometimes teams work exclusively with one another. They make commitments just as they do in marriages. But some collaborations are more casual, and both partners work with other people. My advice is not to focus on what you *don't* do together, but on what you *do* accomplish together.

If your partner is suddenly successful with another writer, it is natural for you to be jealous. Your partner, however, is also the co-author of many of the things you wrote, and his success is contagious. So be happy for him, acknowledge his victory, be gracious about it, and use it to give the songs you do write together a boost.

Nobody can explain why one collaboration works and another fizzles. I try to give each new association a fair shot. It doesn't always take in the first song, so try three tunes together. You'll know by then. It's either magic or it's mediocre. Period. If an old partner of yours is suddenly successful with someone else, figure your turn with your current hit-writing partner is coming up, too, and keep working.

Sometimes collaborations are a matter of convenience. You may be the only two musical people in your zip code. At first you were both in the same place in terms of your career-you had everything ahead of you and nothing but enthusiasm for your team effort. But suppose you find that your partner isn't holding up his or her end of the bargain. Maybe your collaborator is not as committed as you are to being a hit songwriter anymore. Maybe your partner is writing the same melody sideways every time you get together. Or suppose you've just outgrown your co-writer professionally. Maybe your melodies have been steadily improving, but his lyrics aren't. What a difficult dilemma to be in! Suppose you've pushed and encouraged your partner to dig deeper and come up with something more original. And suppose it still isn't coming.

This is the time when you have to suggest you both try working with other people. Don't sever the relationship permanently, because your present partner could just be going through a slump. Something could happen in his or her life in six days or six months to trigger that spark of greatness. But you owe it to your songs to make them as good as they can be. Tell your co-writer you want to work with some different collaborators to try to stretch new muscles in your creative life. Put the onus on yourself, not your partner. You know in your heart when your collaboration is working. When it isn't, you have the choice of either being victim to it or taking charge of it. The people with hit songs take charge.

This breaking-up process can be very tricky, especially if you write with either your spouse, your roommate, or a relative. If you think working with different collaborators will damage your personal relationship and if you feel that is more important than your songwriting career, fine. Stay where you are. But if your career is important to you, you have to muster the courage to be honest. If your mate is really rooting for you, he or she will understand and wish you well. It shouldn't have any effect on your personal relationship. I always feel I can bring more to a partner when I'm the most fulfilled and satisfied from other sources. Then I bring that fulfillment to the collaboration. It makes our time together even more satisfying. And it also gives me an identity away from the relationship, which is vital to me, allowing me to make a unique contribution to that partnership.

If you choose to stay with a partner you know is holding you back, eventually your resentment will contaminate the collaboration. I could make a long list of clients who were very creative but unsuccessful before they came to me. They were squashed from living or working with the wrong person. Later, when they ended their negative relationships, these same "squashed" songwriters blossomed into miraculously successful hit writers with other co-writers.

You may not realize it, but writing is a risk. Moving on is a risk, too. But without taking chances, we'd all live boring, safe, predictable lives. Songs can't be boring, safe, or predictable. They should be inventive, exciting, and right on the edge. Being a creative person involves taking risks every day of your life. Be aware of it and make your decisions accordingly.

♪ WORKING WITH A COMPOSER

When I write without a melody as a guide, I have too much freedom. I may write something that is articulate but dull from a rhythmic point of view. I tend to use too many syllables. While I know better, there is a part of me that wants to paint a more vivid picture in the lyric or describe an emotion in greater detail. Then I end up with long lines of fifteen or sixteen syllables each and wonder why my collaborator can't come up with a melody that sizzles. So for me, being in the room with the composer and writing simultaneously works best. That way, I don't go off on any tangents, and my partner doesn't have to go through my lyric eliminating all my hard-sought adjectives.

Obviously this process works best when I'm collaborating with some-one I trust. That means I can suggest a terrible line or phrase and not worry that my partner is going to think I can't do any better. I may come up with forty turkeys, but my partner knows from past experience that idea forty-one could be the gem we've been waiting for all day.

Trust is the major ingredient in any successful collaboration, because you give each other permission to risk being bad. You know how to deal with the near misses. You've learned from your past experiences together how to urge your partner on in a new direction when he or she has been stumbling with the same stuck melody or lyric all day. Trust. Without it, you are auditioning, not writing. You should write from strength, not fear. That is just as true when you write and compose by yourself.

Whichever method of collaboration works best for you, it's vital for you to understand the subtleties of the relationship. Then if something isn't working, you can stand back and be objective. Ask yourself: "If my friend was having this problem, what would I suggest he do?" Take your own advice. In a successful collaboration you shouldn't try to dominate or control another person. Your job is to write hit songs. The songs are what count. You have to do what is best for those songs. Ultimately what's best for them will be best for you, too.

When I collaborate, I try to set the appointment for the time when I am most creative. In my case, it's first thing in the morning. While I could jump out of bed and immediately address Congress, I find out what my partner's best time is and try to compromise on what's good for both of us. If he or she is a night person and wakes up at four in the afternoon, that signals trouble. But as professionals interested in doing what's best for our songs, we try to find a balance. Then I do creative exercises to get ready, so that when I walk into my partner's office, I'm set to work and don't have to waste an hour revving up.

The most successful teams are made up of people who have respect for each other's craft and for each other's time. You are equals. Remember that. On the first few occasions in my life when I worked with "stars," I felt so insecure that I wrote badly. But now I write feeling like a star myself. I'm pumped up and ready for anything. And on my best days, I write like a champion. If you feel insecure, your partner will feel the same way. Then instead of ending the session with a hit, you write a disaster. If necessary, trick yourself into feeling confident. Keep repeating, "I'm a terrific songwriter. I have something unique to say, and this collaboration is working!" Pretty soon you *do* feel confident, and your partner picks that up and you're on your way.

Tell your partner what you expect from him beforehand. It's not fair to be suddenly furious with him for lapsing into yoga on the piano top if he didn't know you find such behavior unacceptable. Too many songwriters seem to be on day passes from the Home for the Nearly Normal as it is. Each person has different expectations. It's always best to check out your collaborator's quirks in advance. Do your homework. Make the collaborative experience as comfortable as possible.

♪ PARTNER OR EMPLOYEE?

A song used to have two parts, the words and the music. However, since almost every tunesmith has access to software called Pro Tools, we can make very slick, sophisticated recordings at home for very little money. Record companies and music publishers are used to hearing full-sounding demos that really aren't demos at all but can be used as masters. So the "ears" of the music industry have become much more demanding in terms of the quality of our productions.

Because of this, songwriters who aren't producers face a quandary: should they include the recording engineer as a co-writer? I have heard stories that they do, and I have heard stories that they don't. I've been presented with this myself and feel that the engineer is adding the track under the song, yes, but didn't write it, and therefore why should he be listed as a co-author? However, the production can make or break a tune, and if you're a prolific writer, paying a producer could certainly break the bank. So as an incentive to the producers I hire, I pay them a generous production fee, and if the work they create starts getting recorded, I also give them a bonus to keep them interested. On occasion, I have added a percentage of the publishing to their professional fee. Truthfully, a great track is absolutely essential to making a good demo or master, especially in dance, R & B, hip-hop, and rap. So you can hold on to 100 percent of your publishing and 100 percent of your writing, but with an iffy production, that often adds up to 100 percent of nothing. If, on the other hand, you give your demo producer 10 percent of the publishing as a bonus, he'll do better work, and your 10 percent will be very well spent.

What I often do is tell my engineers that although the songs we're recording are demos, if and when they ever become masters, we'll bump up their fees and have them participate in the sync license for the movie, the TV show, the commercial, or whatever it is. And I insert a sliding scale into our agreement. *Of course, everything I ever do is in writing.* Please develop this habit, too.

I never work for nothing, and would never expect anybody else to work that way, either. The world is full of talented recording engineers who have been asked to forgo their creative fees in favor of a percentage down the road. But down the road seems to come and go, and they never see a dime. So if you want somebody to do his best work for you, pay him what he's worth.

I'm not a techie and never will be, and I have to laugh at myself when I'm writing a new song, and *finally*, finally get the melody right, and the words just so, and agonize over the chords—*without* sleeping and *with* too many gingerbread cookies. Then I make an MP3 of me singing the song a cappella, which is really a treat, especially for the deaf. I refer to this as the "Molly Demo." And send it to the singer who's going to record the song so she can tell me what key is best for her. Then I send the MP3 with her key to my engineer. After that, I go around the corner and down the hill and meet with him for an hour or so, going over the arrangement I hear in my head, telling him how I want the song to sound, because how I *hear* it and how I can actually *play* it are two different things.

Like me, and like you, all creative people are very sensitive, with fragile egos. I have to be careful to phrase everything just right, making sure that everybody on my recording team feels good and important along the way. I only hire professional people who do excellent work and give me and my client their best. But occasionally I run into some brick walls that no one in any other business would ever believe.

For example, my engineer never answers his telephone. He has voice mail, but it gets full, and he doesn't care if people can't leave messages because he doesn't like the phone. The ringer is always turned off when he is recording, and he always seems to be recording. He figures if anybody wants to communicate with him, he'll get an e-mail.

I, on the other hand, hate e-mail. (That started when some yutz with my surname, from whom I hadn't heard in twenty-two years, sent the following message: "Mother's dead. Funeral was today. You're not in the will. Regards.") It's probably no coincidence that to this day, writing e-mail kills my neck. Besides, it usually takes twenty e-mails back and forth to say what you could say in a two-minute conversation, right? But, no, my engineer is sticking to his story, keeps his voice mail full, and we go round and round and round. At first, I got really upset about this, ranting, "The man is completely whacked. I should just find another producer who answers his f'kakta phone!" But this guy is talented, knows my shorthand, and we make a good team. Once in a while, to encourage him to listen to his voice mail messages and make room for new ones, I bake a fresh batch of brownies, put them on a lace doily and a very nice plate, drive around the corner and down the hill to leave the goodies under a green Styrofoam bunny outside the engineer's door. Under it, I place a note saying, "Please call me." Sometimes the engineer does, sometimes he doesn't. Oy. That's our process.

The reason I am telling you all this is because the recording engineer is a very important part of the song collaboration process. Over the time period during which we've worked together, he has become a little looser, and I've become a tad looser, too, and the bottom line is we have dozens of great songs to show for it. Although I am paying him well to do what I ask him to do, his input and feedback are very valuable to me. He always does a work vocal, just to show the "real singer" where the words go, and I've actually gotten a message from him saying, "I would never sing that line. I would never say that to a lady." And that's very valuable feedback. Most people are intimidated by me when it comes to songwriting and wouldn't have the guts to suggest what I'd written wasn't perfect. But I really respect input from a colleague, and respect is a critical ingredient to a successful collaboration, no matter who is collaborating with whom. If everybody in the partnership does his best work and gets the best work back from his writing partners, then they can expect the songs they write together to have that much more magic and momentum and a much greater chance for success in the marketplace. It's not just about throwing a tantrum, smashing all the windows on the block with golf clubs, and getting your way. It's always, always about doing what is best for the song. If you are writing with somebody who doesn't feel that way, you are writing with the wrong person. Period.

Songwriting is my professional priority. I am not a member of the United States Senate, I don't sell Miele dishwashers, and I don't do left-brain surgery for fun and profit on long weekends. I am a songwriter. I live and breathe songwriting, and I'm committed to doing my best work every time out, making sure I haven't slipped a little here, or that something slides there. My clients deserve my very best every time, and I only work with people who bring that same integrity and energy to the table.

However, a few years ago, I found a singer who had a phenomenal voice and sang my feelings better than I felt them, so I started using her to do my demos. Her name was Puffy. She and her husband, Pete, had a recording studio in their home. He was cutting the tracks for me and she was doing the vocals, and we were doing good work together.

During the recording of what must have been our tenth song, a monumental breach of ethics occurred. I had a client on the East Coast who wanted to be at the recording session. He flew across the country on a non-refundable ticket to do so. I told Pete as well as Puffy that our date could not be changed, and asked them to please be really careful about scheduling things around our time so my client wouldn't get to town and find out that there was a problem. And as many times as I had reminded them of that, maybe half a dozen, sure enough, the day of the session, as my client landed in L.A. I got a call on my cell phone saying Puffy had taken another gig and would have to postpone ours.

My client had already landed in LAX and I had been on Highway 101 heading to the studio for an hour when I got this phone call. To make a long, sad story short, we finally got the vocal done and the song turned out okay, but I felt it was important for me to tell Pete and Puffy how upset I was that they disregarded and disrespected the value of my client's time and money.

As long as I have been in the music business and as long as I have been dealing with dysfunctional people, I've never had a phone message like the one Pete left, saying they really wished I would bring more professional people to their studio who could understand when something more important came up. To this day, I am still shocked that they would dismiss my client's feelings, and mine, with the fact that it was *our* problem for not being more professional!

So that was the end of that collaboration. I couldn't possibly put any of my clients through that again. Even though I was a steady customer and paid everybody very well, upfront, for everything, the agenda of the singer and her husband was the singer and her husband, who had complete disregard for me and my clients. That is totally unacceptable. It doesn't take long to discover why very talented people never achieve the success they deserve. And the sad part is they're never responsible. It's never their fault. It's always somebody else's.

When this happened, it felt like a death to me, that I had lost the production arm of my company. But after a lot of long walks, most of which were uphill, and several bags of York Peppermint Patties, I realized that the world is full of great singers and talented engineers, and I found a new team. The only people I want to work with value me, my business, and especially my clients.

Some collaborations last forever, some for the weekend, some don't even make it as far as the first chorus. But that's how it is with creative, sensitive people and our artistic projects. It's devastating, absolutely devastating, every time a writing/production team splits apart. But it's part of the process. You move on, leaving your sadness along the way to the next song and the next. And down the road, when you strike gold collaborating with someone new, you realize you never would have written that song if you hadn't been dumped by the hottie with the holes in his purple socks who sang like an angel, but forgot that you wrote the tune.

Collaborations should be overhauled every few months, just like cars. If you haven't evaluated your musical relationships lately, here are some questions to help you do that.

Collaborator's Check List

1. Are you happy with your collaborator? If so, why?
2. Are there areas in your work together that need improving? What are they?
3. What do you think you can do to improve your working relationship?
4. What do you want your collaborator to do to improve your working relationship?
5. How long have you worked together?

6. What success have you had as a team?
7. Do you think it's impossible for you to reach this level of success or beyond with anyone else?
8. Does the thought of a change scare you?
9. Do you see yourselves as partners in ten years?
10. How do you get over your crises as a team?
11. Is there someone else you'd prefer to work with instead of your partner?
12. Is there someone you'd want to work with in addition to your present partner?
13. Are your songs as good as they can be? If not, why?
14. What can you do about it?
15. What do you like best about what you bring to the collaboration? List ten things.
16. What do you like best about your partner? List ten things.
17. List twenty-five reasons why your partner should be happy writing songs with you.
18. List all the ways you can improve your writing relationship together.

6
Making Time to Write

know what it's like to have great ideas surging through you but no time to write them down. Most songwriters have other jobs. Those jobs are usually time-consuming and draining. Then when you get home, you have families and bills and landlords and laundry to deal with, so when do you get time for yourself? How do you make room for your songs?

To me, songs are like children. If your child was in need of your time, wouldn't you give it to him? So give your songs the same consideration. Whenever you're torn, keep thinking of your song as something you created that brings you pleasure but needs some of your quality attention. You know it will give back to you everything you give and more.

We're all plagued with voices telling us we're not writing. Even when we *are* writing, the voices tell us we could be doing more and doing better. That is the critic at work. Usually writers wrestle with this critic until they understand his dynamic and develop a system of controlling him.

When I finish a writing session, I tell myself out loud that I did a good job, that a few great lines are a terrific start and I should be very proud of myself. This kind of affirmation helps to drown out the critic who will never give you credit for doing anything right. You have to learn to recognize this guy. He's seductive. First he'll tell you that you've *got* to work today. He nags you until you can't procrastinate any further. Even when you get down to your song, he judges the value of what you've put on paper—all negatively. When you finish your daily assignment, you probably are thrilled and full of joy and pride. But this guy goes right into high gear and challenges you. ''Okay, so you've got a song. But who in the world's going to sing it? Who ever heard of you?

How are you going to get this to an artist who means something? Maybe you should just throw it out with the garbage."

Obviously this critical voice is destructive. What you have to do as a professional writer is acknowledge its presence but remember that you have two ears. In the other ear, you have the creative, purely inspired voice telling you that what you've done has a great hook, is exquisite, powerful, emotional, lasting, and meaningful. And as you do with a stereo system, you can learn to adjust the volume of the critic's voice so your own supportive voice broadcasts louder.

Writers who don't have time to write envy writers who do. But let me share a secret with you. Writers who have all day to work welcome distractions so they don't *have* to write. I've found that what works best for me is to schedule an appointment with myself to write, just as I would schedule an appointment with a publisher, a beautician, or a masseur. I can't change or cancel the appointment. I set aside time from my day for the writing process. I mark it in my appointment book—in ink. I only write during those hours or minutes. I don't take phone calls or answer the door while I'm working. I don't allow any interruptions. Once I make the commitment to spend this time writing, I honor it. It'll work for you, too.

I'm most creative early in the morning. If I weren't a writer, I'd make a great newspaper deliverer. I find if I get out of bed and go directly to work, I can put in a couple of good hours before the phone starts ringing—before people and other responsibilities start invading my day.

But I'm a morning person. Some of you are comatose until noon. And then you're at work doing your day job. How do you concentrate there? And when you get home from work, the baby's crying and the older kids are throwing mud at your wife. You'd kill for a hot shower, but the power has been turned off because you spent too much for your software and the Con Edison people don't consider your music a priority. Where in the midst of this chaos are you going to find time and space to write love songs?

First, create a place for yourself where you can shut out all distractions. Maybe it's the basement. Perhaps it's the garage. Or maybe it's the backseat of your car in the garage. I have one client who sits on the floor of her closet with her terrific, inexpensive portable keyboard and headphones. While it's probably more practical to have a separate room in which to work, those of you who don't might look into the closet approach. It certainly is private.

Set down rules. You are not to be disturbed, except in case of fire. Even then, if it's only the kitchen that's in flames and you're in the bedroom, leave word with the firemen not to noodge you unnecessarily until you complete your time commitment to yourself.

If finding peace in your house is impossible, go to a park or a coffee shop. Take your portable keyboard and guitar and your notebook, and plan to spend twenty minutes there, deliciously alone. Nobody doesn't have twenty minutes. You may not have two hours, but you *do* have twenty minutes. With just that short span of time ahead of you, you'll be excited to take advantage of it. You'll be amazed how productive you can be. No matter how successful we become, it's still better to wish we had more time to write than wish we had more to write about.

As important as it is to make time to work, it's also essential for any successful writer and artist to know when he or she needs a day off. A woman I used to know was one of the busiest and best screenwriters in the world. She was in great demand and was always working. But once every ten days or so, she took a day off, got a roll of quarters and a large box of Tide, and headed out on a laundry run to visit her three children, all of whom were in boarding schools within a couple of hours drive of Los Angeles. The change of agenda was very valuable to her, since she always came back filled with stories of the road and experiences of her kids that exasperated but at the same time nourished and enriched her.

Focus and commitment are essential to your success, but so is time away from your work once in a while. You need new experiences to write about and keep you balanced.

A writing teacher of mine said he liked to take his notebook to museums, where he would park on a bench and work in the crowded halls. He claimed the more noise he had to drown out, the deeper he would have to concentrate. He came up with ideas he wouldn't have gotten if he had just stayed home and didn't have to focus so sharply.

One of my clients, who is from a farm in Texas but now lives in a tiny, crowded apartment in Long Beach, can't work at home. He needs more space to feel comfortable writing. What he does is drive to the parking lot of the Queen Mary with his guitar and write for two hours in his car. He also follows every writing session—no matter how productive—with a chocolate espresso. Whatever works, do it.

I've noticed that when I have the least time to write but have set aside a few minutes to *try* to write something, I get the most done. When I remove the *demand* from the task, the part of my creative ego that has been squashed with "shoulds" can flourish. You wouldn't expect to come up with a killer title or a great hook with just eleven minutes left before an important meeting on some other project, would you? But that's when I do my best work. When I'm seeing clients and have only a small part of each day to work on my own songs, I write infinitely better than when I have the whole day ahead of me just to write. One good, productive hour is much more valuable to me than a whole day of mediocrity. Like many writers, I suffer greatly from isolation. While I resist it, I can spend six or eight hours alone at my piano or desk if I know I'll be seeing somebody after I finish work. Consequently, I schedule a lot of dinner dates. It works well for me. You can try it, too.

Let's go back to your park or coffee shop. Say you put in your twenty minutes. Now you have to be back at work. Chances are you've got something new on the pages of your notebook. You may not think it's what you were after initially, but you have something. Be sure to check off in your appointment book that you kept the meeting with yourself to write that day. This way you acknowledge you met the commitment. You know you've spent twenty minutes writing and you have words and notes on a page to prove the time was productive. You reluctantly head back to your job, wishing you could just stay put for another half an hour and get the song finished.

Your reluctance to end your songwriting session is normal. But you'll have something to start with the next time you schedule an appointment with yourself. Besides, while you may think you've stopped writing, your subconscious knows that's false. It never stops. It's like one of those twenty-four-hour 800 numbers. There's always someone on duty.

I think of my mind as being much like a computer bank. It has information stored away on files that may be hard to retrieve. But if I send in a request for information (notice I didn't say "demand"), the little microchips in my brain take the request and then seek out the file containing that particular information. While I think I'm just driving my godson to the baseball-card store or picking up clothes at the dry cleaner's, my subconscious is on red alert, seeking out the new ideas for which I left a request earlier in the day or week. And when I'm watering my plants or baking, an idea will suddenly come to me. Of course I write it down. And if I haven't the time to address it right then and there, at least I have something to start with for my next writing appointment.

I work best when I write every day. Even if it's just twenty minutes at a time, I try to write something on a daily basis. That way I'm always ready to write. I don't have to spend my precious writing time warming up the way I would if I had missed a day or a week in between writing sessions.

I don't always write songs. Sometimes I'll write a little letter to myself reminding me how well I did the day before. Sometimes I'll write a note to the gardener begging him to save my gardenia bushes. I might rewrite that letter nine times. But the point is, no matter what I'm putting on paper, it's all *writing*.

No matter what is on the page, I always try to enjoy the writing process. I constantly make it fun for myself. If I feel stuck on a serious, intense love song based on a true-life adventure, I'll scribble four lines all rhyming with "zickle," which is a silly-sounding word and one I've never used in a song, just as an exercise to warm up.

I recently returned from a marvelous trip to Martha's Vineyard and had to write a thank-you note to my host and hostess. I was so exhausted and jet-lagged my first day back I couldn't compose even a brief letter that didn't sound hideously boring. What made it worse was knowing that my host was a sensational writer. Both he and his wife are world-class wits, and I knew they were expecting something other than "Thanks for the hospitality. Love, Molly." So instead of a traditional, socially acceptable thank-you note, I wrote them a thank-you limerick. I had fun with it. I fulfilled my social commitment. I used words I'd never been able to use before in songs. I felt accomplished. And with the rush and satisfaction from that brief five-minute exercise, I was then ready to work on a love song.

I prefer to write for two or three hours every day, but during my busiest periods, when I'm lecturing across the country, I find my writing time gets whittled away until I'm left with only Sundays for uninterrupted writing. This used to be catastrophic. It ranked right up there with the plague and having to go to traffic school—again. But now I've learned to trust myself to use that time wisely and well. I know from past experience that when I just have a few hours, I perform brilliantly. That gives me the courage and incentive to take what I *do* have, pull out all the stops, and go for it.

With all the lectures and seminars I give, I find myself spending more and more time on planes. For some reason I'm always on the toddler flights. I honestly think the airlines gather up children—the cuter the better—and arrange for them all to be crying at the same time so I can't concentrate.

I was a baby once myself. But I can't walk up and down the aisles singing "Mary Had a Little Lamb" all the way to Omaha. So what I do is lock myself in the bathroom. I know it may sound selfish, but with four or five hours during which no ringing telephone can disturb my writing process, I intend to make the best of my time in the air. Even if there weren't babies crying on the planes, there are always flight attendants conspiring to ply me with Pepsi, little square chickenettes, and reconstituted pea pods. Being in a tourist-class seat is no place to write. Not for me anyway.

I've done well in the lavatories of the friendly skies. There is no place I've ever been that is more uncomfortable or more crowded. There *is* absolutely nothing else I can do in there to distract myself. So when I enter with my notebook, I come out with songs. The flight attendants are often concerned about me, but on leaving I smile and assure them it was just a touch of the *touristas*.

Please note that with the exception of my recent trip to Martha's Vineyard on a nine-passenger Cessna (there was no bathroom on that aircraft—they replaced it with a chapel), I only fly on large planes. So there's always more than one bathroom. I'm not recommending airplane lavatories to everyone—it just happens to work for me.

For those unscheduled bursts of inspiration, always keep a pad and pencil next to the phone, in your pocket, purse, and car. You never know when you'll be stuck in traffic for ten minutes. Instead of leaning on the horn like your fellow drivers, you can be working on a hit song.

Always keep a writing pad and pen next to your bed. Our subconscious minds are the most free just before we drift off to sleep. Don't let a good idea get away because you're too tired to go get your writing pad. Never trust yourself to remember it in the morning. You won't.

You should also have a separate notebook just for titles and ideas. That way, when you're feeling a little dry, you just have to open your book and the ideas you gathered on more inspired days are right there waiting for you to develop them.

Please do me one major favor. Promise me that all of your notebooks will be ring-bound so your precious pages can't be torn off or fly away. I never trust my ideas to yellow legal pads. (Lawyers might, but I don't trust them, either.) It's too easy for loose-leaf pages to get lost. Ideas are the only resources I have. So each time a notebook is full, I put the date on the cover, just like I do on my checkbook, and file it. That way I have every draft of every song I ever wrote. If anyone ever wants a rewrite (and they always do—even if the song's already been a hit), I have all of my alternative drafts right there.

I believe ideas fly through the air into our minds. If we don't think enough of these ideas to commit them to paper, they'll get insulted and fly out of our heads into someone else's. So cherish your inspirations and be sure to keep careful track of them all.

However many days per week you write, be sure your appointment book reflects that total at the end of the week. Add up the hours. Keep a running tally. There's a tremendous sense of accomplishment in knowing you put in the time and kept your commitments. You will also come to realize that with all that quality time spent in writing, great results are imminent.

You should reward yourself after each writing session—even if the session only lasts twenty minutes. The creative part of our personalities is a child. And the child needs a reward. Give it to him. Then next time you want to trot him out to work, he'll remember you took good care of him, bought him a surprise, and made it fun afterward. So he'll be more willing to work with you next time if you take good care of him now.

Writing a little every day is like oiling machinery to keep it functioning at a high level of efficiency. I was advised to run the air conditioner in my car for a few minutes once a week even during the winter to make sure the system will work when I need it on hot, muggy summer days. I pass the same suggestion on to you about your writing. I know it works.

For those of you who have time to write but don't use it for writing, it could very well be you just don't *want* to write at present. Maybe you should spend the time reading or gathering new experiences to write about in the future. The creative process cannot be compared to working on an assembly line. There, you have to show up for work each day and put together a required number of widgets within an eight-hour period. But as a songwriter, you will have days that are seemingly productive and others that aren't. On the ones that aren't, give that time to yourself anyway. If you've set aside an hour to write and have a blank page when it's up, at least write, "I kept my appointment with myself today. I'm very proud of myself. I've finished writing for today and my subconscious will take over from here. It has never let me down. I expect surprises in the wind."

There's a few lines right there, see? And it's all nurturing. Nothing is harder on a writer than that awful, persistent, nagging critic's voice saying you're not doing it correctly or you're wasting your life, throwing away money and time you could spend more wisely on other things. Shut that voice up. He's a bad guy.

In the case of one client, the voice was so loud I told him to give it a tangible form and put that object in a drawer while he wrote. He decided it was an ugly old dirty ashtray. He put it in his upper-right-hand desk drawer while he wrote. When he was finished, he took it out again and showed the ashtray he had written something wonderful. Trembling at first, he steadily gained momentum and control until he finally overpowered the bad guy. Now he doesn't listen to his critic much anymore. With practice, you'll be able to overpower yours, too, and the time you make to write will be well spent creating hit songs.

At the end of each writing session, answer these questions:

1. Did you get a good idea today?
2. Did you write it down in your permanent notebook?
3. Did you make and keep an appointment with yourself to write today?
4. Was it a productive session? List everything you accomplished: verse, chorus, bridge, title.
5. When is your next appointment with yourself?
6. What have you done to reward yourself for honoring your time commitment and your good work? List three things.

In the end, an artist has to be his own good parent. Make peace with that and act accordingly.

7

Stimulating Creativity

Some of us are lucky. We have so many sparkling, exciting, fresh ideas, we'll never run out. But others may find from time to time in their creative lives that they're going a little dry. If you find you've been writing the same thing sideways in your last several songs and your melodies are all starting to sound alike, it's natural to feel nervous and a little frightened for your creativity. You swear you're doomed to spend the rest of your life wistfully remembering the exhilarating days of fire and thunder when you were getting great ideas and writing hits.

But you *can* do something about it. You don't have to play victim to your muse. You can be inspired by another one. Here are some exercises that my successful clients and I have done when we're feeling dull, sluggish, and unable to squeeze anything memorable from the air.

First, you should recognize that the creative process is cyclical. While your subconscious never stops working, your conscious mind *does* need a day off now and then. Use this time to gather new experiences instead of staying home, groaning, and beating yourself up.

Get out of your house or office or wherever it is you usually write. Close the door to that area, both figuratively and literally. Head for a place you've never been. I usually go to the same restaurant for breakfast every day. But when I'm stuck and feeling stale, I change my pattern. Instead of wearing my comfortable old sweat suit and meeting people I already know, I put on eyeliner and my best new clothes and go someplace where I don't know anyone. In a foreign environment I see new things. I feel new things, hear new things, smell new things. Instead of my usual peppermint tea, I might have a café au lait or espresso. My taste buds are treated to new experiences.

Eavesdrop. If people are talking about the stock market, don't ignore them, thinking your songs are about love, not economics. Listen to what's being said, even if you're way over your MasterCard limit and your checks are bouncing. If nothing else, you'll learn something, hear some vocabulary you normally don't use or think to use in love songs. Your brain will store these words and phrases. I believe that for every new idea our brains receive, a little red neon sign flashes in the gray cells that says, "Interesting, stimulating, give me more." And the devoted librarians at the conservatories of music in our minds file it all away in the appropriate departments.

Strike up a conversation with a stranger. Make up a new identity. Tell your breakfast partner you're a pediatrician or a test pilot or the social secretary for the governor's wife. Become that person for twenty minutes. Don't worry if you blow it. This is a game. It's supposed to be fun. But whatever you do, don't sit there and pour out your heart to a stranger about how stuck you are. The point of this exercise is to give yourself some time off from your problem, not to compound it.

Go to a museum. Force yourself to look at works of art you might have avoided during earlier visits. You might not like Byzantine art, but check it out anyway. Not long ago, I was feeling as creative as a soggy mop. I went to see the French Impressionist exhibit from the Hermitage and Pushkin museums in Russia. Not only was I totally delighted by the art, which is from my absolutely favorite period, but also I stumbled onto a Lalique exhibit I didn't even know existed. I left, my mind dancing with ideas, raced home, and worked until midnight when my back quit.

So if your brain has been running on empty, realize it needs input. Give it what it wants. You don't know how it'll assimilate that information or use it later on. As a sensitive writer, you're like a vacuum cleaner. Your job is to absorb new experiences so you feel alive, enthusiastic, excited, interested, and stimulated.

Go into a store you've never been in. Look at merchandise you'd never consider buying, which might be aluminum siding or the Hope diamond. Listen to the salespeople talk. They're funny. They don't need to know you're there with a secret motive. You may not need a new Ferrari just yet. Go into the showroom anyway. Act as if you're a serious buyer. Observe everything, including the other customers.

Check out the sales pitch. See about financing. See if they'll take cash. Check their responses. This is your persona. You can handle it any way you want.

A successful stimulant that works for me is going to a different supermarket. At my regular one, I know where everything is. In fact, I could probably go through the place blindfolded and still find the peppermints and pâté. But when I go to a different market, I don't know where anything is. I might get mad and be tempted to walk out. But the discomfort of being in a strange environment is actually very stimulating. Once, I was in an unfamiliar market and was fuming because the checkout person was on 33⅓ rpm and I was on 78. But while I waited, I saw a guy with a walkie-talkie and a calculator. His children had a food list, as well as walkie-talkies, and they were calling in prices from other aisles. He'd enter that price on his calculator to see if they could afford that item in their weekly food budget. And they were talking like truckers—using all that "ten-four" jargon.

I loved it. I didn't care that it took forty-five minutes to purchase one pint of low-fat milk. The experience was worth it. It gave me tons of ideas. While I haven't actually used a man with a walkie-talkie and a calculator in a supermarket in any of my work just yet, that's okay. I was distracted, amused, and entertained. The experience was rich and will always be with me.

♪ CHANGE THE MENU

Speaking of supermarkets, I think we all tend to buy the same food items from week to week. So buy a couple of new items—things you've never tried. If that's too big a step, let me suggest you simply try a new brand. I know the tendency is to go with the familiar and the comfortable. But this exercise is meant to jostle you up a little, to take some risks, and to have some new experiences as a result.

We do have our principles. No matter how stuck I am, I'd never buy anything other than Heinz ketchup in the squeeze bottle. Period. But I'm willing to bend in the fruit juice section. Why just a while ago I bought Minute Maid apple juice—at a substantial saving, I might add—instead of my usual Motts. It felt weird. I wondered if my metabolism would change from the new taste and I'd suddenly become tall and willowy. But see, here I was thinking about that instead of my poor, doomed song. So the exercise worked.

♪ THE DICTIONARY GAME

It's important to have a little routine to do at the beginning of every day to make you feel that you have lots to say and an unlimited source on which to draw. I suggest you try the dictionary game. It was recommended to me by a poet, and it has never let me down. The game only takes a few minutes and can be a lot of fun as well as very enlightening.

To play this game, open your dictionary at random. Drop your finger down on the page. Choose the closest *picture* or *proper noun* to your fingertip. Write it on a piece of paper under the column heading "Nouns." Make sure the noun is not one you use regularly in your songs. If you land on "love" or "loneliness" or "heart," keep your finger moving down the page until you find a more unusual word.

Find nine more pictures or proper nouns in the same fashion. Make sure you don't get them all from the same letter in the dictionary. This an equal-opportunity exercise. Stop when you get ten nouns. Then do the exercise ten more times, choosing adjectives you've never used in a song but would say to someone in conversation. Write the adjectives down in a column next to the nouns. Match each adjective with each noun.

Write the results on another piece of paper. Then cross-pollinate each noun with each adjective. Somewhere in this list of pairs you will stumble over something you've never thought about before. You could find a terrific title. You could find a great phrase. You could assimilate the beginning of a song. The rhythm of the words might suggest a melody.

If you get things that don't make sense, like "reindeer detergent" or "polyester pie," don't throw them away. You might want to try writing a silly song, maybe even a commercial for a fictional product. You use the same creative muscles to create a silly song as you do in writing a love song. You just have unusual subject matter. If it's fun and seemingly stress-free, you won't make the same demands on your writing that you associate with "real" songs and it'll whiz by, making you feel you're on a hot streak.

I give this assignment to each of my new clients and they have fun with it. Remember, writing is supposed to be fun. As the second part of this assignment, take one of the pairs of words from your lists twice a week and write a stream-of-consciousness story about each of them. Write down whatever comes into your head. Never mind spelling, punctuation, grammar, or logic. It can be as whimsical or romantic as you let it be. I recommend you introduce the element of magic and the unexpected in your story. One of my clients recently found the phrase "crackerjack Porsche" by playing the dictionary game, and it sparked a story about a shiny red Porsche that ran on Cracker Jacks, not gas, and so instead of zooming down the street the way those cars normally do, this Porsche bounced like popping corn. Another client found "sizzling redhead," but instead of writing just another story about a hot-looking woman who seduced him in a bar, he wrote a saga about a guy who was a frustrated melody writer who couldn't give away his songs on Earth. He was taken by this sizzling redhead to a planet where they didn't have any songwriters—just programmers who designed rhythm tracks, and nobody had anything to sing. On this planet, everything he wrote was a hit. But then, bored with easy success, he hitchhiked home to Earth. It was a marvelously creative experience for my client, who'd been feeling stale lyrically up to then, and it opened up a hot creative streak for him that hasn't stopped yet.

If you play the dictionary game every day before you start work, you'll find yourself with exciting new things to think about all the time. And with new things to think about, you'll certainly have unlimited material to write about. That way the blank page won't be your enemy, but your ally in helping you to get this endless flow of ideas committed to paper.

♪ YELLOW PAGES

Something I do when I'm feeling a little stale is flip open the Yellow Pages, and wherever my finger drops, I call the number to ask about the services that company offers. I've learned about beekeeping, coin collecting, skylight installation, and all-night dentistry. Gathering this information has the same effect as playing the dictionary game. It makes me think about new things, it's terrifically stimulating, makes me feel like I've had a little adventure, and just takes a few minutes.

♪ REROUTING

For a quick exercise out of the house, next time you're headed some-where, take a new route. You'll see things on streets you've never seen before. Next time your car is in the shop, instead of bemoaning your lack of wheels for the day, take a bus. In Los Angeles that comes under the heading of science fiction. We usually just rent another car. But taking the bus puts you in touch with a whole new realm of experiences. You'll come in contact with people you wouldn't ordinarily meet. Observe them. How do they dress? What do they say? What are they carrying? Do they wear hats? Did they have bus passes? Did they know the driver? Did they speak English? Check everyone's shoes. What shape are they in? How many people are wearing sneakers?

Once I had to borrow my neighbor's van. Driving it after my Rabbit convertible was astounding. Riding up that high made me feel like a trucker. I assumed a different persona. I was Molly Belle, the singing teamster, on my way to Chattanooga with a load of chickens. I drove like a maniac. It was an adventure. When it was over, I was glad to have my little Rabbit back, but I was invigorated from the experience.

As creative people, we are both drawn to and afraid of new things. If we can learn to overcome the fear, we can jump into new experiences. With our curiosity about the world unleashed, we'll never be stuck for new ideas.

♪ PHYSICAL EXERCISE

Since writing is cerebral, doing something physical works wonders for stimulating creativity. Some people jog every morning. While they're jogging and sweating like mad, their whole bodies are stimulated and invigorated. When they're exercising, these people focus on different objectives—completing that two miles or five miles or even just making it to the corner. The point is, they have short-term goals that are physically demanding but have nothing to do with writing.

If you do your five miles, you usually feel a sense of completion and pride and can then move on to the next task at hand—writing. Accom-plishing something physical the first thing in your day is a wonderful way of warming up for cerebral exercise. Completing one thing gives you courage and incentive to start another.

I don't jog—I walk. I'm not lazy. I have a delicate lower lumbar region. But I still do my hour of exercise every day. I used to have a set path along which I walked every morning. Now I find deviating from that path is a lot more stimulating. Lately I've been drawn to the ocean and marked out a four-mile path along it. Currently you'll find me at sunup walking through the alleys of Santa Monica, because this week I'm having rural longings. Being unable to take a vacation just now, I trick myself into thinking I'm in the country by taking the alley route, which looks just like back roads. When I come home from my walk, I'm invigorated both physically and mentally. I take my shower and I'm all ready to write.

Though I tell myself I walk for my health, the truth is it gets me out into the world where things are going on. I can't imagine stumbling over much of interest in my kitchen, unless I've been trying to cook again and something explodes. I have to go out into the world, rather than expect the world to come to me. While I'm walking, admiring the flowers and the birds and wondering about the psychological differences between those of my neighbors who build fences and those who don't, my subconscious is at work, too, clearing out the cobwebs and getting ready for a good day at the piano or the computer.

♪ MEDITATION

While I may wake up ready to write in the morning, I reach a lull about midday. In order to get myself over that hump, I take the phone off the hook and meditate for fifteen minutes. During that time, I try to stop all the thoughts that have been rushing through my head like race cars on a complicated freeway system and envision only white space. I am not doing this to "get" anything, merely to give my mind a rest. I make the same commitment to meditating that I do to the rest of my work, and nothing can interrupt me.

When I first started to meditate, it was difficult making the time and sitting still that long. But like anything else, the more you do it, the easier it gets. Now I look forward to the peace and tranquility of those fifteen minutes as much as I look forward to my oatmeal in the morning. I find I'm overtaxed and cranky if I don't meditate. And I always feel refreshed and re-stimulated afterward. This is a keeper. I recommend it highly.

The wonderful thing about the brain is, the more you know, the more you want to know. It's not like a closet that gets full and closes down. A successful man once told me, when you want something done, ask someone busy to do it. That's because there's an energy, a rush that goes with activity. Somebody whose machinery is already oiled and pumping is ready to go to work. So if you're revved up with interest about the yen/dollar ratio, it is contagious and helps you with your love songs, too.

The bottom line is this: try new things, go to new places, talk to new people, try new foods, drive new cars, drive down new streets, and constantly change your life patterns to allow for new experiences, which will continually surprise you. You will have new things to think about and write about with renewed enthusiasm, energy, excitement, and vigor.

When you're feeling uncreative, dull, and listless, here's a checklist you can use to help get back on track.

1. Did you do any exercise today? Meditation?
2. Did you play the dictionary game or the Yellow Pages game?
3. Did you take a bus or other form of public transportation?
4. Did you drive down a different street or shop at a different market? Go to a new restaurant and try something unusual?
5. Did you create a new, temporary persona and have him/her talk to a stranger?
6. Did you go to a museum?
7. Did you write a nonsense song or limerick'?
8. Did you peruse a newspaper or magazine you normally don't read?

If you get all nos, choose a couple of items from the list above and do them. If you get all yeses and you're still stuck, I think you definitely need to fall in love. Nothing will give you more inspiration. If you're still stuck after falling in love, break up. That'll do it.

♪ YOGA

I started practicing yoga after all of the stretch classes were canceled at the Sports Club L.A. because yoga was trendier. Swell. I attended grudgingly because I didn't think I could do the elaborate moves the practice demanded. I mean, hey, I've never been to an ashram, I get altitude sickness, so I'd never survive in the Himalayas, and I didn't especially like that unpleasant purple yoga mat color. But I had an expensive membership, and my body needed to be stretched. Son of a gun, in addition to getting a wonderful workout, I found that as I did the yoga poses, and especially the breathing, for the hour or so I was in the class I was really thinking about yoga and nothing else, which is unusual for me. My mind is usually racing and bouncing off ninety-three things. But in the yoga room I was simply in the yoga room and could honestly feel I was present.

However, there has never been a song on which I was stuck or a problem in another part of my life that didn't get resolved during a downward dog or a sun salutation. So it's very interesting to me that while I practice yoga to get away from my concerns, and give my mind some peace, the solutions to all of my issues seem to come to me while my mind is completely relaxed.

If you are not a yogi or yogini yet, I suggest you try a class or two, unless of course the instructor insists on playing that mellifluous "I am a hyena being sawed in half" CD, so popular on the central coast of California these days. I practice yoga every day, and no matter what else is going on in my life, I make time for it. I'm very grateful for the peace I find from the practice, and especially the phenomenal positive energy I feel between me and the other students in the class. Although they don't know what I'm thinking, or what my mishigas is that day, I truly feel their support in solving the concerns I'm facing, and I'm sure they feel my support with theirs. In this chaotic world, where I am actually afraid to turn on CNN, it's really important for me, and you, as artists, to feel peace and positive energy. Without it, there wouldn't be any songs at all.

If you prefer jogging, great. Biking? Excellent. Just do some form of exercise for at least twenty minutes each day to keep your heart pumping and your blood full of oxygen. The hits are often hiding in stretched muscles. You can take that to the bank.

8
Overcoming
Writing Blocks

No writer, no matter how famous, prolific, rich, adored, quoted, industrious, or disciplined, hasn't faced, at one time or another, the terror of not being able to write. There is nothing as devastating or debilitating as that hideous feeling. It's like taking a euphoric glider flight across wine country and then suddenly being flung from 20,000 feet without a parachute onto the terrain below, which has somehow turned to sheet rock.

I've been there. I've overcome it. I've been back and lived to tell about it and proudly show off the glorious pages of work I've done after the battles were over. If I can nurture myself through this agony, so can you.

Writer's block is caused by fear or anger or both. Every dry spell in my life can be traced back to one or the other. It's as though they go out for a drink and leave you there in a puddle of screaming mush wondering what the heck happened. You were doing so well this morning! You feel frantic, doomed. You are lost forever. You're never going to write again. Your only hope and salvation is a "real" job, with no demands. Just show up at nine, leave at five. Answer telephones, polish shoes, and that's it. You're not a writer. It's over. Forever. Amen.

Does any of that sound familiar? I bet it does. You might have seen me at the newsstand, searching seriously through the classified sections of seventeen daily papers, circling ads for clerk typists. Maybe you've seen me buying the GRE study guide so I could go get an MBA and have a real life. Or you saw me purchase a dozen "how to" books containing strategies on earning a million dollars a month on mail-order suppositories and software in my spare time. Sound familiar? Or did you perhaps catch my act as I grabbed copies of every magazine from *Barrons* to *The Singles Register*, looking for a kind tycoon who'd take me off my own failed hands and marry me?

But I'm in good company. Every successful writer has crashed into this abyss. On bad days, I can see the shadow of Oscar Hammerstein II across the street from me, climbing the oleander trees, preparing to jump in front of a big blue bus careening down the Berkeley Street hill. I think I've seen Shakespeare in a sweat suit down at the park along the ocean, ripping pages out of his notebook and muttering to himself like a bag lady. It's entirely possible for a songwriter who won a Grammy last year to be unable to write a note for the cleaning lady this week. Crazed, he grabs his award and heads for the trash bin. But a kid on a skateboard comes by whistling a tune our songwriter wrote and the crisis is over. A little recognition makes it all go away. The songwriter turns on his heel and runs to his piano, where he proudly places his Grammy again and begins to write a new song.

What would you do if you saw a barefoot, freckle-faced, four-year-old kid in a striped T-shirt and a Dodgers cap sobbing on your doorstep as his ice cream falls into the street? You'd take him in. You'd want to comfort him. *I'd* want to hug him, rock him in my rocking chair, maybe lend him my teddy bear, kiss him on the forehead, hold his hand, and tell him it's going to be okay. I'd buy him another ice cream cone—two scoops. I'd take him to a toy store and tell him he could have anything he wanted. Absolutely anything. I'd read him a wonderful story and tell him repeatedly how special he is. I'd pamper him. I'd protect him. I'd surprise him. I'd make this the best day of his life.

Each of us has a lost four-year-old inside of us, making demands when we are blocked on what I call "midnight afternoons." Make a list of fifty things about this poor kid. Describe him or her in precise detail. Here are some questions to ask yourself to help get you started.

1. What color is his hair? Is it curly or straight?
2. What color are his eyes?
3. Is he crying?
4. Is he missing any teeth? Which ones?
5. Is he skinny? Chubby?
6. What language does he speak? Does he lisp?

7. What is he wearing? Describe his clothes in detail.
8. Did his mother abandon him?
9. Did an older kid steal his baseball cards?

Keep going. List fifty more things about this poor child. When you're finished, you'll see how needy this kid is and how terrific you can be to make it all up to him. That kid is you. So now take care of and comfort yourself just as you would the child. Make a list of twenty things you can do to pamper yourself. Then do them.

If you can learn to do that, you will learn how to take care of the frightened child inside you and make him feel safe again. People who feel safe can move on. They can take chances with blank pages. People who feel safe assume their ideas are good. People with good ideas write them down. People who write down good ideas keep finding better ones and eventually find a great one they want to run with. They nurture it. Structure it. Refine it. Rewrite it. They finish it. They reward themselves for that victory. Then they write something else.

♪ GETTING READY TO WRITE

A lot of writers misinterpret their "prewriting" phase as being writer's block. They're simply getting ready to write. Any writer who wants to be good to himself has to learn to recognize his own personal, eccentric, and often ridiculous warm-up.

Each of us has a pattern of preparing to write, and if you recognize that pattern, you'll see you are making progress instead of thinking you're regressing. I used to get terribly upset with myself for not being able to take a beautiful, rhythmic, world-class tune and simply sit down to write the lyric. I had to do the following things first:

1. Plug in my heating pad and put it on my bed at precisely the right angle.
2. Arrange the pillows behind my back just so.
3. Get my thesaurus and rhyming dictionary.
4. Get comfortable with being in the room.
5. Get myself a cup of peppermint tea.
6. Get myself something to dunk in the tea.

7. Get myself another cup of tea that didn't have cookie dunk floating in it.
8. Find my other MP3 player.
9. Find my title notebook.
10. Find my current writing notebook.
11. Search for my gum.
12. Search for my lucky pen.
13. Make another cup of tea.
14. Rearrange the pillows.
15. Call everyone I knew on the planet and say I was going to write and ask them not to disturb me (even though I had a voice mail that could pick up on the first ring).
16. Put on my lucky lavender socks.
17. Go out in the rain with a ten-cent-off coupon to buy new tea bags on sale eighteen miles away.
18. Return home via a new route that took longer.
19. Boil the water for my new, bargain tea, but decide on a diet soda instead.

I used to think that while I went through each of these steps I was not writing. I beat myself up for wasting all that time, which in some cases was as much as an hour or two. What I didn't realize until later was that all of those distractions were really part of my *warm-up* process. I needed to go through each of those steps before I was ready to write, before I felt safe enough and comfortable enough to take the risk and dig for something new.

I've worked hard to recognize changes in my warm-up process. And most of the time I have a pretty good grip on it. At one time, I couldn't begin a project without a box of animal crackers handy. But some days I need french fries. There aren't any in my pantry. That means getting in my car and finding the nearest drive-through restaurant. At five in the morning, they can be scarce. Nonetheless, as the menu changes, so do my writing and warm-up habits. Rather than saying I'm procrastinating and not doing what I should be doing (all those ugly words parents used on us), I've learned to understand what I am doing, to figure out why I'm doing it, and realize that it's just part of the deal I made with myself in order to work.

In the case of the french tries, I finally realized that I needed to get out of the house for a little while before I started to work. I'm never not writing. I'm always getting *ready* to write. The semantics make a difference because one is a positive, nurturing statement; the other is punitive. So be careful how you phrase things. Learn to say them so they sound positive.

As an exercise, make a list of all the things you did before you last had a productive writing session. Don't leave anything out. Even making love or taking a shower or doing a push-up while making love in the shower or tweezing your eyebrows or brushing your teeth count. So does vacuuming and gardening. And car washing, dental flossing, ironing, reading *Playboy* or *Playgirl* or both. Polishing your toenails and eating sushi are also valid, although not necessarily in that order. Write down everything you did. This is not for publication. It is an exercise. It's therapeutic. Nobody but you will ever see it. So don't censor a single step. When you have your list, you'll see what you need to do to get ready to write. Do everything on that list, in order. I think you'll surprise yourself. You might just feel like writing.

But keep one important thing in mind. You didn't get blocked over night. And you might not get unblocked that quickly, either. You have to work through it. Give yourself the time to do that. I know you're impatient and feel you have to get back to work. But if you really want to solve this problem, give it time. By putting too great a demand on this unblocking process, you're just creating a new series of frustrations.

I often find myself washing dishes before I start to write. I have a dishwasher, so why do I do this? Because the warm, soapy water feels good. It's very sensuous and at the same time safe, because I'm controlling the situation.

Another thing I've noticed I do now before starting to work is vacuuming. I have a housekeeper, so why do I do this? I like to see immediate, tangible results. And I do see them. The carpet is clean. The pile stands up straight. I did that. I controlled it. Now I can take charge of the thoughts and words lining up to pop out today.

♪ FEAR

If you're stuck, make a list of things that frighten you. Or if you claim nothing does, then try a list of things that make you uneasy or uncomfortable or worry you a little. Things that might happen if the Big Earthquake comes or if the stock market crashes. Come on. You're a neurotic writer. Go for it. There must be something you're afraid of.

What about getting old? Oh, the perennial favorite, being alone forever and never achieving your songwriting goals? Does that strike any terror chords yet? Huh? Should I keep going or have I shaken you up enough to get you in touch with some of the things you really are afraid of? List them, in detail. Nobody will see this but you. Nobody's going to laugh at you or tell you you're imagining things.

Here are some suggestions to get you started:

1. Is there something you have to do that makes you a little uneasy?
2. Did somebody say something flippantly that caught you off guard and made you question your ability?
3. Do you think you've peaked?
4. Are you worried about earning a living?
5. Did someone imply you're just another writer and are in no way unique?
6. Did he say it in jest, but do you now wonder if he wasn't kidding?
7. Do you worry that your friends are doing better than you are?
8. If you're a writer with a contract or assignment, do you think they won't like what you hand in?
9. Do you think they'll buy you out of your contract and dump you?
10. Do you worry they'll hire someone younger and smarter in your place?

Now elaborate on what you're afraid of. Use scraps of paper if you want to. Or a fresh notepad. Or type it. Just list every detail of your deepest fears.

Then beside each item on your original list, write what you can do to remedy your fears. Your response to question three, for example, could be, "I'm writing better every day and I haven't peaked at all." A soothing response to question five would be that you're a very, very special writer, and in spite of what someone might have said, you're a hit songwriter. Go down your list of fears and put a soothing comment next to each one.

There. You've faced it. It's not gnawing unseen and unknown in your gut anymore. You know now what you're up against. Now you can fight back using the soothing statements you've already written.

♪ ANGER

If you're blocked and you're not afraid, then you're angry. It will help you get to the source if you ask yourself these questions:

1. Are you furious?
2. Totally aggravated?
3. Mildly disturbed?
4. Somewhat annoyed?
5. No? Not even with a neighbor who parks his car too close to yours and dings your fender?

Aha! What are you mad at? Who are you mad at? What happened last week that still has you grinding your teeth? Maybe three months ago somebody said something and today you choose to address it. Do you see what I'm getting at? Things happen to us. As sensitive people, we've developed mechanisms to cope with the things that happen to us. But they clog up our lives.

As with fear, you have to describe your anger. Pick up your pen and write down why you're mad. Write it in letter form if you choose—and pretend you're really going to mail it to the person you're mad at. You can use as many four-letter words as you want. You can forget punctuation and spelling, too. Tell everybody off. It's the best of all possible situations because you get to speak your mind and you're safe. Nobody can get even with you. If you don't want to write it down, talk it into a tape recorder and then play it back—loud. You are purging your soul.

People who are free of anger can feel gentle things. When you're happy, you can let go and let other things happen to you. When you're not mad anymore, you have time to *feel* something else—to *do* something else. You can refocus your energy and find out what's going on in the world. Now you're open and receptive. You're curious about everything. You could just be reading the newspaper; an article might spark an idea for a song. You write the idea down in your notebook. You find another idea that goes with the first one. Pretty soon you have several ideas that could be included in a package. You get a title. You move the words around a little and you get a spectacular title. You write it down. You write it all down. You are writing again. *You are writing again!* You finish the song. You rewrite it your required number of times. You use it as proof that you can do it—and do it again!

Once, I was horribly blocked and in desperation went to Karin Mack, who gave a class at UCLA in overcoming writer's block. I learned the root of my problem was anger. I mean serious anger—leaking in from almost every aspect of my business and personal lives. Karin, who, co-authored the excellent book *Overcoming Writing Blocks*, knew I was a songwriter. She suggested I go home and write a sonnet for each person or situation infuriating me. I should tell you that before I met Karin, I hadn't written a syllable in three months.

I went home and sat down at my kitchen table at 5 P.M. By midnight I'd written fifty-three sonnets. That's how mad I was. They weren't Shakespeare, you understand, but they were sonnets. I had no rules to follow other than to make each sonnet fourteen lines long and end with a rhyming couplet. Karin suggested the sonnet format since it was a *form*, and I was used to writing within certain guidelines. I was allowed to use four-letter words. Yeah? Well, I was so riled I even made up new ones. The feelings I got down on paper were ones that I couldn't express to my publisher or my boyfriend. This sonnet outlet was perfect. I was surprised at how much anger there was inside me that was unexpressed. Occasionally a phrase popped out that was pretty good. So I purged my soul and at the same time regained my courage to create.

♪ WARDROBE

When I write, I often wear an old sweat suit, and by the end of the day, there are cookie crumbs all down the front of it. My hair looks like it's been nuked, and the mascara from the evening before is somewhere down around my nose. I might even have a hole in my lucky lavender argyle socks. But on those days when I don't feel like writing or looking that unsavory, I wash my hair and style it perfectly, put on my going-to-tea-at-Trumps makeup, try a new eye-shadow combination, unwrap a new pair of fancy pantyhose, and put on the new outfit I'd been saving for a very special occasion. Then I make a deal with myself to go into my office. Just for five minutes. To tidy up papers. Before I know it, I'm sitting at my desk, hard at work and loving it. What I do is make a happy occasion out of writing, instead of the same old monotonous routine. Dressing up will work for you, too.

Whether you're blocked or simply have a long warm-up process, I hope you realize now that it's perfectly natural for you and all other successful writers to take side roads and detours to get to your writing. I don't care if you could've gone from A to B in three seconds. If you went from A to Z and then back to B, and B was successful, who cares about the trip to Z? Give yourself permission to have your warm-up time. Once you do, your writing will come a lot easier. You'll be in a much more positive frame of mind when you start, and that can only lead to more positive results.

9
Getting Your Songs Published

Each week when my assistant opens our e-mail, she finds as many as one hundred missives from new writers wanting to *sell* their songs. We also receive fifty phone calls on the same subject. It's important for you to know how the music business works so you don't make catastrophic mistakes early in your career, get discouraged, and lose interest completely in using and sharing your very special gifts. *Songwriters don't sell songs.* We get them recorded and are paid when they are performed or when copies of our songs are sold.

In the traditional music business, a songwriter or singer/songwriter approaches a music publisher in the hope that the latter will be excited about the work and champion its creator. For a writer who doesn't sing, that means, ideally, the music publisher finds an artist or artists to record his songs, and for a singer/songwriter, the music publisher will help him secure a deal with a record label.

When songs are recorded, they earn royalties, which, for all intents and purposes, are split equally between the songwriter and the publisher. If you draw a circle, putting a line through the diameter, you will have two equal halves. The songwriter's royalties are the top half of the circle, and the publisher's royalties are the bottom half.

In the traditional music business, songwriters make money from three main sources: (a) mechanical income, which is from the sale of records and downloads, (b) from performances for profit whenever their music is performed on the radio, the Internet, on TV, and in all concert venues, restaurants, and bars, and (c) when a song they write is licensed for use in a movie or TV show. The mechanical royalties are paid by the record companies to the publishers, who in turn pay the songwriters their share. And the three performing rights societies, ASCAP, BMI, and SESAC, monitor performances and send quarterly royalty checks directly to the songwriters and music publishers, who also distribute licensing fees to the writer. Since so much music is being stolen on the Internet, mechanical income has dwindled down to almost nothing. However, performance and licensing income has skyrocketed. Although the Internet has killed one income stream, it has produced hundreds of others, many of which are still in their infancy, but nonetheless are creating new ways for songwriters and music publishers to make money.

The music business has been highly criticized and is paying a terrible price for trying to put locks on its music, attempting to prevent piracy and theft on the Internet instead of facing it as a reality and finding new ways to make money from music. The same thing has happened to the movie studios. After spending billions of dollars putting water-marks and locks on their films and swearing that nobody could steal them, it was discovered that when a new movie opened at 1:00 P.M. on Friday afternoon, by 1:01 P.M. the entire film was available for free downloads on the Internet. The same is true when a CD is released.

I asked some of my colleagues what they felt was going to happen to all of us and to the work that we produce. David Ross, president of Music Row Publications, says he's 110 percent pro-copyright. "We finally saw the realization creep in that digital rights management wasn't going to work. Until now, we thought we could run the Internet like a Wal-Mart. Lock it up at night and exit single file by the cash register. However, the Internet is designed to make the transfer of information possible. There are no encryptions or digital locks on music anymore, and no restrictions on MP3s. Our industry is finally in step with the reality of what is. Before you solve a problem, you have to come to grips with having the problem. You just can't lock these songs up." In spite of all of this, most music publishers are getting record multiples for the sale of their catalogs, so the overall health of publishers is better than ever because of performing rights and synchronization rights, the latter being when a record or a song is used in a film or a TV show. That end of the music business is booming.

Dan Rosenbaum is vice president of advertising music and catalog development at Cherry Lane in New York. He told me the music industry is truly in a transitional phase comparable to the introduction of radio, the 78-rpm record, and then the long-playing "vinyl" album. At each of those junctures, more people were able to hear more music, more of the time. The status quo tried to maintain its dominance, but was outsmarted by new players or visionary "old schoolers," who realized how to work with and benefit from the new technology at hand.

Dan says, "What is startling now is how quickly it brings new possibilities for music distribution. First it was the iPod, then mobile phones, now social networking sites. Each time a new business model has to be developed, it makes it very challenging and at the same time exciting to be part of the industry.

"In order to thrive, the record labels and music publishers have to be ahead of the curve. This is why you see the real innovators on the landscape coming from the independent, or "indie," sector. They're not as burdened by the more traditional ways of doing business. Now with the Internet and mobile distribution continually offering new possibilities, the smaller, more nimble companies can afford to try things out, see what works, and move on to the next possibility far more easily than the larger, multinational labels and publishers.

"There is a related development going on in the advertising industry, where the thirty-second spot, for almost sixty years the preferred way of reaching the widest possible audience, is, for all intents and purposes, dying the same slow death as music distributed as physical records. The large, multinational agencies, controlled by larger entities called holding companies, have found it difficult to move nimbly in a new frontier, where first TiVo, DVRs, and now mobile distribution, along with increasing competition for audience attention from video games, have given the public at large ample opportunity to *not* watch a commercial. Again it's the smaller agencies, often dubbed 'boutiques,' who have led the way with new and less costly ways to reach a brand's targeted audience, moving advertising away from the all-encompassing thirty-second spot."

Dan went on to say, "The Web is a positive tool financially for writers because (a) it opens up so many ways for downloaded recordings to be sold, and (b) offers greater possibilities for tracking those purchases. Video games are now designed so that a player can purchase a song he hears as it's playing! This is an unprecedented and potentially huge source of income for songwriters.

"Take a look at what's around you—where are people hearing their music? Right now, the most successful writers will target at least part of their efforts on the areas where songs are now heard by millions—television, film, video games. They will take advantage of what the Internet has to offer. A few years ago, no one had heard of MySpace. Now you can start a network there of fans around the world."

Bruce Broughton, an old friend and Oscar-nominated film composer, told me, "I see the Web generally as a positive tool for music creators. It's a good way to get one's music out on one's own steam. I know many composers, arrangers, and songwriters who have gotten a substantial audience of listeners and music purchases simply by using a MySpace page. Many personal Web sites now make it easy to download music, both as audio and as written sheet music, for purchase. Whether this personal effort is as worthwhile as the wide distribution a substantial publisher can offer, I couldn't tell you. I only know that many people are doing it, easing some of their frustration of not being able to connect with or be signed to a substantial publisher, as well as giving themselves a sense that they are somewhat in charge of their own creative lives. Ring tones are a comparatively new market for songwriters and composers, which is huge. YouTube is another."

♪ MARKETING

Writing the song is only part of your job as a songwriter. Now you have to get it out into the marketplace where it can be heard and start generating income. That doesn't only mean setting up a MySpace page, or putting your songs on iTunes, and waiting to be discovered. You have to be with the folks in the real world, outside your house, and meet as many people in the real music business as possible, face to face, not just online.

First, test-market the song. Play it for several objective listeners for input to see if there are any glaring errors. An objective listener is someone who isn't automatically going to tell you it's great even if it isn't. He or she is someone who's knowledgeable about what's on the charts and who can constructively criticize your work.

You should develop a support group of other writers and musically inclined friends for whom you can play all your work on a consistent basis. Remember, you are writing because you want to share your songs with the world. The world will never hear them if you don't make your material accessible. You need constructive criticism all along the way. Believe me, it's better to get it before you demo the song than after, when you've spent days in the studio and hundreds or even thousands of dollars on a song that nobody is interested in.

Assuming there are just a couple of rough spots and you've taken the time to carefully rewrite the song to eliminate them, you are now ready for the next step: making a demo.

♪ THE DEMO

A demo is the recording you make to demonstrate the song. These days it has to sound like a master. It doesn't seem fair, but that's what the situation is, and knowledge is power. With the easy access we now have to home studios and software that reproduces the sounds of almost every instrument, it's easy and practical to make a full-sounding, master-quality demo for just a little money.

Some of the best recording software programs are: Abledon—Live, Propellerhead—Reason, Cakewalk—Sonar, M-Audio—Pro Tools, and Steinberg—Cubase.

Publishers and producers used to be content with a simple piano or guitar/voice demo, but now they've come to expect masters. Leikin's law is to give them what they want. Produce demos that can compete. Make yours as close to master-quality as you can.

Publishers rarely spend money on demos anymore. It doesn't seem fair, but again, it is the truth. Deal with it.

But what do you do if you don't own a studio or Pro Tools and you don't have the technical chops to make your own demos? And what do you do when people advertise online that they can record your songs for you for $199? When something sounds too good to be true, it usually is. I can't tell you how many thousands of bad demos I've heard that have come from tunesmiths who've used their kids' college funds to hire companies that pander to naïve, new writers. The product is terrible at best, and there is no possible use for it except as a very sad, expensive coaster.

It's ironic that when you need shoes, you go to somebody who makes shoes, but when you need demos, the last thing you should do is go to a studio that only makes demos. It's been my experience that companies cranking them out all day long have an innate, burned-out aura about them, and you can tell from listening to their work that they just plain quit trying to be real producers in the real music business. It's very sad. God bless them for trying to make a living. But when I make my demos, I find a studio and a producer and an engineer who can translate what I hear in my head into a digital format that sounds like the Top 10. People I work with record CDs and jingles and soundtracks, too, so producing an individual song or two for me every now and then is a treat for them, not a chore, and I know that every single one of my songs sounds professional and competitive.

But, you say, you're not me, and you don't have my connections, and you don't know my studio guy du jour. No, but I would be happy to share my recommendations with you, so call my toll-free number and let me hear what you need. I can usually help you put just the right production team together to do a really good job, get you what you want and what you need in order to realistically compete in the marketplace.

I always work by recommendation only, so I would never use a studio unless somebody I know and respect referred me there. I ask to hear work that is in the style similar to the one in which I write, and I ask how much that recording cost. I also like to speak to the person for whom the recording was made, and I don't mean exchange e-mail. I mean a *real conversation*, simply because it is too easy to have a bogus e-mail address and pose as someone else.

I think of my songs like my children. Nothing is too good for my children, so nothing is too good for my songs. I am very hands-on when it comes to the recording of my work. While it might be nice to write a song and send it off to some studio in cyberspace and not give it a second thought, that puts the songwriter in a victim position. It's important for you to take charge of your songwriting career, which includes the recording of your demos. And if you know nothing about the process, learn it—that's part of your job. Again, don't be a victim. Choose your studio carefully, and remember, just because it happens to be in Nashville doesn't guarantee it's good. Yes, there are lots of fabulous production houses in 37212, but I know guys in garages in the Cucamonga Wilderness who are brilliant producers, too.

Imagine for a moment that you're sitting across the desk from you, and you're the publisher, and you've heard 300 songs already that day, and know there's a major artist cutting in a few days or a week or even a couple of hours. You are desperate to hear something that's dazzling, that gets you dancing on the desk, and more important, will inspire the people you have to pitch the song to. They include the artist's manager, producer, and the artist himself. You need a song the record label is willing to spend hundreds of thousands of dollars promoting. So you have to give the music publisher something that's gonna blow the basements out of every building on the block.

♪ CONTACTING PUBLISHERS

I'd like to open this section with a story. A music publisher and four friends who were not in the music business were out on a yacht in a choppy sea. The boat suddenly capsized in the storm. Sheldon the shark came by and gobbled up four of the men instantly. The music publisher was untouched. When asked later by his fellow sharks why he let the music publisher go, Sheldon replied: "Professional courtesy."

This is how songwriters usually feel about music publishers. Actors have the same reaction to their agents. And it's a fact of life. We need each other and we hate each other. We don't think our publishers are doing enough. They think we're asking too much. They feel we're morons and envy our creativity and freedom, and we think that they've had lobotomies. Unfortunately, I doubt it's ever going to change, so get used to it.

Contacting publishers requires a lot of persistence. Music publishers are inundated with songs and overwhelmed by the demands made on their time from people they already know. So when you approach someone cold, be prepared for resistance. Don't take it personally. You can't be offended when someone who doesn't know you or your reputation doesn't jump. Accept their behavior as how they treat everybody and keep on trying.

Subscribe to *Billboard* magazine. It is published weekly and lists all the hits on every chart. Along with the title of each hit song, the name of the publishing company is listed along with the artists' and writers' names. So if you think your song is right for a particular group, find out who published their last hit and contact their publishing company.

If the group writes its own songs, don't bother submitting material there. They probably won't listen to outside material, let alone record it. Some artists are so lawsuit-prone, they're advised by their attorneys never to listen to anyone else's songs—especially someone they don't know.

So be smart about submitting material. Before you go to the trouble of trying to penetrate a busy publishing office, make sure all the acts they service aren't what we call "self-contained," recording songs they write themselves.

Assuming a group isn't self-contained, call the publisher of their latest hit and find out who their professional manager is. That's the guy who screens material. Check the correct address with the receptionist, telling her you need the information for your updated Rolodex. Then say good-bye. When you have a list of twenty professional managers and companies compiled, *then* start your serious calling.

Your initial call will go something like this:

RECEPTIONIST
[dithered]

Bigtime Music!

YOU
[charming]
Hi! Who is this I'm speaking to?

RECEPTIONIST

Why?

YOU
I'm a songwriter. My name is (fill in your name).
What's yours?

RECEPTIONIST

Please hold.

You're on hold. Stay there. She'll be back. Eventually.

RECEPTIONIST
[still dithered]
Bigtime Music! Hold on!

YOU

But . . .

Keep holding. Don't get mad. Stay calm. The little lady has all her lines flashing at once. Be her friend. She could use one.

RECEPTIONIST

Bigtime Music!

YOU
[quickly]
Hi! I'm (fill in your name).
And you are?

RECEPTIONIST

The receptionist.

YOU

Right. And a *very* good one. But what's your name? You have a lovely voice. I'd like to know who I'm speaking to.

RECEPTIONIST
[softening a little]
Sherrysue. Please hold.

And you do. You've got twelve seconds left on your calling card. But you keep holding.

RECEPTIONIST

Bigtime Music!

YOU
[quickly]
Hi, Sherrysue. It's me (fill in your name). I'm a songwriter. I have a hit for Miley Cyrus. Nobody else in town has heard it yet. Since I see in *Billboard* that your company published Miley's last single, I'd like to meet with (the professional manager) and see if we can do business together and make some money.

                    RECEPTIONIST
Can you hold?

You're dying to strangle the woman, but you keep your cool. You need
her. Finally . . .

                    RECEPTIONIST
      Yeah?

                         YOU
Sherrysue, like I said, I've got a *hit* song right here
for Miley Cyrus and—

                    RECEPTIONIST
We don't listen to unsolicited material.

                         YOU
                    [confidently]
Hey—I know. But this isn't just another
unsolicited tune. I met (professional manager) at
a seminar a few weeks ago and she asked me to
call as soon as I had something recorded. I'm a
professional songwriter, Sherrysue, and I'd like
your help and cooperation in putting me through
to (professional manager).

                    RECEPTIONIST
He's in a meeting.

                         YOU
When could I call back?

                    RECEPTIONIST
He's going to New York tonight for two weeks.

                         YOU
Okay. I'll give you a call a few days after he gets back.

                    RECEPTIONIST
But then he's going to Guam and Helsinki . . .

Although you want to put your fist through a wall, you bite your tongue, take a very deep breath, and cheerfully say you'll call back again. And you do.

In Molly-Ann Leikin's *Master Class in Songwriting*, a good chunk of time on the MP3 series is devoted to being gracious and forceful on the phone. It's an art. Work on your telephone craft as much as you do your writing. It's a big part of your job. You've already worked hard and sacrificed a lot to create those great songs of yours. Don't they deserve that extra push to get them heard? Call the Sherrysues of the world back. Keep leaving messages for the professional managers. And since they probably won't return your calls, you keep calling them. Eventually they'll crack and ask you to send in a CD or MP3. Push for a face-to-face meeting. Otherwise your song will be listened to on the run in a stack of a thousand and will have no chance whatsoever. You didn't come this far to get a form rejection letter, or e-mail with the word "passes" in the subject line and a list of the songs they aren't using.

So work on your telephone persona. It should not be the same person who created the songs, but someone you put on, like a brand-new, smartly tailored suit. Your business persona is irresistibly persuasive, charming, assertive, *and* persistent without ever being obnoxious. Work on this persona until you've got your "act" down.

You might even want to give yourself another name while you're making your business calls. When I'm feeling too vulnerable to call as Molly because of some past difficulty with a particular person, I call as "Sally," my assistant. Nothing they say about Molly or about being too busy to speak to Molly ruffles my feathers. I am gracious, understanding, and I always get what I want. Sally has no emotional investment in the business at hand and can take as much rejection as anyone can dish out. She's cool. She's calm. Above all else, she is professional. When you can behave in a totally professional way, you will triumph on the telephone.

♪ POWER PHONING

Developing confidence on the phone requires practice. As an exercise, try calling the chief executive officer of a major corporation. Say you have an idea for his company that will make a lot of money. See how far you get and how many underlings try to intercept you en route. Remember, you have nothing personal at stake here. Your only goal is to reach the CEO. He doesn't know you. But you must speak to him to complete this exercise. Once I got the highest-ranking general in the air force to call me back. After that, I realized it couldn't be all that difficult to get through to a publisher at Warner/Chapell Music. I want you to feel that confident, too.

♪ PREPARING FOR A PUBLISHING MEETING

Let's assume that after calling back twenty times and insisting (without threatening to slash the tires of his Porsche) that the professional manager makes an appointment to see you, you've arranged to meet him at his office. Prepare a CD on which there are no more than three songs. Please don't go on safari through a ninety minute CD for a song while in a publisher's office. Don't bring him a bad copy with a long explanation, either. Neatly type all your lyric sheets. Put your name, phone number, and the name of the other writer(s) at the top of the page and write the following at the bottom of the sheet:

© (Year) Your Name.

And that's all. Don't write "Member of ASCAP" or "Member of Texas Music Association" or "Runner-up in the Wyoming Watusi Festival 1945." It reeks of amateurishness. Please—just put the information I suggested.

While this might appear inconsequential, one client approached me with her lyrics typed on a typewriter that had fancy script type. It was impossible to read because the printing was so small. It was also so curlycued I couldn't have deciphered it even if the letters were bigger. This is not an invitation to the cotillion you're submitting. It is a product with which you're hoping to convince someone in power to do business with you. A publisher is in business to make money. You should present yourself and your work as though you are, too.

The same is true for CD labels. They should bear your name, your phone number, and the titles of your songs. They should not have adorable, fluorescent silver and gold notes dancing all over the label or little treble clefs breaking out between the words. Less is more.

You should also have a business card that bears your name, the word "songwriter" after it, a phone number on which there is a voice mail, your address, and that's all. No cute, smiling notes or darling little treble clefs here, either. Spend your money on a good demo—not on a fancy card.

Don't leave a business card that lists some other profession, even if you're a United States senator, an astronaut, or a Los Angeles Laker. Your card should simply tell the publishers that you are a songwriter and here's where they can reach you.

The former vice president of a TV production company had the most ridiculous business card taped to his desk. It said "John Jones. Motion Pictures, Spare Ribs. The Best of Both." Let me assure you, I wouldn't call him for either.

You can order attractive, succinct business cards at an instant-printing place for $20. There are plenty of businesses online where you can get attractive business cards for next to nothing. There should be room on your card to put a quarter (a twenty-five-cent piece) that wouldn't cover any writing. That means a lot of blank space. People resist reading too many tiny words. Keep this in mind when you have your cards printed.

Dress in what I call "power clothes." They give you a strong, dynamic, magnetic presence in public. Have you ever noticed there are some people you turn and watch as they walk by? There's something about them that exudes confidence. You should be one of those people, whether you're a man or a woman.

I have special "power clothes" I wear just to meetings. They're carefully coordinated in colors that suit me best. My shoes are "showroom new" and well taken care of. My hair and makeup are perfect and my jewelry—even if it's just a watch—is carefully selected to tell the person I'm meeting that I've got it all together, I'm hip, I'm artistic, and I'm unique. You should make the same presentation for yourself. It might take some shopping to find ensembles that feel both comfortable and "powerful" at the same time. But get used to wearing these new clothes and to acting "as if" in them. Then when you really do have a meeting, you'll be confident and ready.

I'd make a point of finding out in advance the kind of clothes the professional manager wears. The odds are he's hip-looking, possibly dressed like nobody you've ever seen before on the planet. I don't know if we're talking orange and purple spikes, but up-and-comers in the music business like to fit in. They often idolize rock stars and dress to imitate them.

If you'd normally wear a conservative three-piece suit to a business meeting, here's where your wardrobe has to be changed. A guy showing up in that outfit will be labeled "a suit" and will be seen as all outsider by everyone in the company. Even the staff lawyer at A&M wore a promotional T-shirt like everybody else. So check out the hot men's and women's "looks" and try to find one in which you are comfortable.

While I wouldn't suggest you spike your hair for the meeting, be aware that you should try to look as cool as possible to *mirror* the person with whom you're having the meeting. If you do, he'll feel more comfortable with you. And that will make it easier for him to like you and your songs.

Be on time. If you've never been to the office before, allow time to get lost. The receptionist is going to be just as hassled in person as she was on the phone. The last thing she needs is a yahoo on her hands who's late and flustered.

While I wouldn't go so far as to suggest you bring the receptionist a rose, I would strongly recommend you make a good impression on her while you're waiting for the meeting with her boss. Ask her a couple of questions about herself. Chances are nobody in the company cares about her. They think of her as a blob with black fingernails who answers the phone. So she'll be flattered by your interest in her. And let's keep that professional. Maybe she's a songwriter, too. Or a singer. Maybe she loves music and is a serious groupie. Or maybe she's just out of school and will one day be president of a major record label. She'll also know the gossip about who's cutting what and the kinds of songs that are in demand that week.

Find out what her story is. The chances are good that in three to six months she'll be working somewhere else, doing something similar or a step up from what she's doing now. If you already have a positive, professional relationship with her, then you'll have an ally wherever she goes. So while you're waiting, be sure to thank her for putting together this meeting. That way she'll feel important and will remember you for it.

♪ THE MEETING

Start the meeting by shaking hands. Ladies, too. No wimpy hand-shakes, please. This is business. Even if the atmosphere doesn't reflect it—music is blaring and Mohawk haircuts are manifesting themselves up and down the halls—this is still a business meeting. The executive preamble that would occur if you were selling lumber or life insurance is appropriate.

Make the publisher feel comfortable. You'd expect it to be the other way around, but it isn't. The first few seconds aren't about music at all, but about sizing each other up to see if you are going to establish a positive and fertile ground for a business relationship. Start by giving him a compliment on a piece of art or a photograph of a child or even an item of his clothing. "Gee, I love that poster." "What a darling child. Is he yours?" These are ways of saying you like and admire him.

Right now the publisher has the power and you want his approval. But don't let him know how much you need it. Act as if this is just another meeting for you. Assume the attitude that you have lots of important people interested in your songs. You've *chosen* to have this meeting with him. Be sure he doesn't know you're seeing him just because nobody else would return your calls.

You want to make a strong connection with the publisher, because you'll be writing songs for a long time. You'll want to come back with your new ones. Flaky, acned, knock-kneed stock boys grow up to be presidents of record companies. Your job is to make sure that when they move up, you move up with them.

Assuming your opening remarks go well, get right into your pitch. Tell the publisher you're a good songwriter. You've studied the craft of writing, you have "holds" on your material by a couple of major pub-lishers, and you've heard good things about his particular energy and way of doing business. You want to work with him because you know you can make a lot of money together. You've also heard that in addition to his being a good businessman and up on everything going on in the industry, he's very sensitive. So you feel he will be able to connect with your material.

Then you play your CD. He may not like the first song, don't get flustered; ask him to play the next tune. If he doesn't like that one either, don't be thrown. Ask him to suggest how you could rewrite it to make it more commercially accessible. Now he's involved with the material. He feels a connection to it—and to you.

Then comes a crucial part of the meeting. It's the time when you have to separate yourself as creator of the songs from the one who is doing the business of marketing them. If the publisher doesn't like your present work but offers an explanation, listen to him. Tell him you hadn't thought of that before, say he's given you some terrific ideas, you appreciate his input, and you hope to see him again soon because he's been a big help to you. Now that you know his tastes in music better, you'll be back when you have these songs rewritten or when you have some new material that falls more into the categories he is most comfortable representing.

If he takes a phone call or a series of phone calls or suddenly needs to look at a magazine, don't take it personally. All publishers do that; I think it's a test. One guy answered five calls while I was attempting to play him a song—a song I'd rewritten four times at his request for no money. I finally mustered the courage to ask him to please hold his calls until I was finished, which would only be two minutes. He said he absolutely couldn't do that because he was in the midst of a big sound-track deal. I shrugged and went on with my song. However, the *next* time I had a meeting with this man, I walked into his office and he told his secretary to hold his calls. So it was a test. Be aware of the dynamic and act accordingly.

Anna Hamilton Phalen, a successful screenwriter, was once trying to tell a story to a development executive at a movie studio, who suddenly picked up a basketball, bounced it a few times on the rug, threw it in the air for a while, and then tossed it to poor Anna, who was in the middle of her pitch. The ball went back and forth between "the players" while Anna tried to maintain some order and passion in her presentation. I know Anna to be assertive and capable of asking someone not to throw things at her—whether she's telling stories or not—but there was something terribly intimidating about this meeting and this particular development guy that prevented Anna from speaking up. So she became the victim.

On hearing this story, I asked Anna what she felt she could've done in retrospect to stop the "basketball game" and regain control of the meeting. I suggested she could've tossed the ball into the garbage pail. But Anna said she should have kept it, twirling it on the end of her finger for a few minutes like Kobe Bryant. I felt she would've made her point with just a little more impact if the finger that was twirling the ball had a perfectly manicured nail at its end.

In retrospect, we were both able to see that the whole thing was a power play. We laugh at it now. But it is unconscionable that a highly professional, successful writer had to suffer like that. When this happened, Anna wasn't some unknown off the bus from Cupcake, Kansas, either. She wrote the script for *Mask*, which had just been released. The film got rave reviews. People were all over Anna like bad suits trying to get her to *come* to meetings. So it wasn't that she was unknown or uncredited. People who hold meetings are often horribly rude. You can't—absolutely cannot—take their behavior personally.

When your meeting is over, shake hands, thank the receptionist by name for her help, leave unobtrusively, and don't fall apart until you're out of the building.

Be sure you do something terrific for yourself as a reward for having had the courage and stamina to get through that meeting. This "gift"—a bouquet of flowers, a box of Jujubes, a movie, a nice dinner at your favorite restaurant, a night with Zena the Zebra lady or Mr. July—will give you more leverage with your sensitive, creative self when you have to set up and go to the next meeting.

After you've taken care of yourself, then you have to rally your objectivity. Write the publisher a personal note, thanking him for his very good suggestions. Say you'll give him the first chance to listen to your next few songs. This personal note should be handwritten on nice stationery. The publisher will no doubt be impressed with it. He spends his life under the gun from people who are usually frantic, uneducated, speak in monosyllabic grunts, and have never heard of Emily Post. This publisher will remember you for treating him with respect and good taste, because that makes him feel like he has some social graces, too.

Now let's assume you've gotten over the rejection from the meeting. You've battled with your ego and have decided to try rewriting the songs. Either that or you're content to let the old ones be for the time being, learn from them, and start fresh with some new material. When it's ready to be shown, contact the publisher again.

Call your old friend Sherrysue. Remind her about the great meeting you had with her boss a couple of weeks earlier. Tell her you have some new material and the publisher asked to hear it as soon as it was recorded. This second appointment should be easier to set up, but it might require as much persistence as the first one did. You don't know what crises may have befallen the company that morning. So don't take it personally if the publisher does not call you back. In a place where six stereos are constantly blaring six different songs, each vying for domination, there are lots of distractions. Keep calling. And keep your cool.

If you still can't get through, try another personal note. Be pleasant, and mention that you've tried to reach him, you have a new song as promised, and you hope when his desk is clear, the publisher will find a few minutes to see you. That usually works for me. In the meantime, while you're waiting for him to respond, call twenty other publishers. I always feel best when I have many options open to me. It's not fair to yourself to let one person's decision to take or not to take your call determine your value as a person or as a writer. But it's hard to separate his not calling you back, for whatever reason, from a personal rejection.

So set up lots of meetings. Assume you've got good songs and you're someone the music publishing world is lucky to be doing business with. Decide ahead of time you won't allow anyone's jammed schedule to put you down or stop your creative flow. When you put out good, gracious, businesslike energy, it'll eventually he returned in kind.

♪ POWER PACKAGE

One way around the difficulty of presenting what I call "orphan songs" to a music publisher is to have your own group. I feel that any songwriter starting out now has to be acutely aware of the state the music business is in. More and more artists are recording their own songs Look at the Hot 100. Ninety-nine of these tunes are "self-contained," which means that you and everybody else who writes are trying to get material to the same one percent. Self-contained groups have producers, friends, or relatives who write. Many of them also have contractual obligations to music publishers. So your chances with them are slim to none.

So create your own vehicle for your songs. Make a deal with a hot but still unknown group you can work with to write for or with them. Be sure they are contractually bound to keep their commitments to you. In writing. Then you can approach any publisher with a "package"—you and someone to sing your songs. Now that you've presented the publisher with an artist, you've just eliminated the hardest part of his job. He can help you get the artist or group a record deal. And then you're on your way.

If you don't know anybody who sings or performs, go out and find someone who does. Search local clubs, high school bands, and talent contests. Be objective. Don't just settle for the local piano teacher or the first cute guy with a good voice who bops along on a designer skateboard. Listen to the radio. Go to concerts. See what's selling. Find an artist or a group that can realistically compete in the current marketplace. It'll require a lot of work, but you owe it to your songs. You want them on the air. This is the quickest and most hard-nosed, realistic way to get them there.

My own experience has shown me repeatedly that just when I've given up on ever hearing from a particular person and have moved on to someone else, that's when the first guy calls me back. I'm inevitably in the shower washing my hair. Of course, I can't tell the publisher this. I let the lather drip into my eyes while I talk business. The publisher will usually apologize for not getting back to me sooner. My job, and now yours, is to make him feel at ease again. You tell him right up front you weren't worried about your project so much as you were concerned about him and hoped everything was all right. He'll appreciate your concern, and he'll be able to tell that you're a serious, business-minded person.

♪ POWER LUNCH

Tell the publisher you'd like to take him to lunch. It's always better to meet a busy man out of the office, away from ringing telephones. No matter how crowded his schedule, he'll still have time to eat. If he isn't free for three weeks, fine. You'll wait. Set a date.

Lunch is a social occasion, but business creeps in and gets taken care of anyway. And treating someone to lunch or a drink makes it your occasion. It gives you power points and makes the other person feel pampered and important. So everybody wins.

Here are a couple of pointers on lunch that work for me. First, ask your guest's secretary where her boss likes to eat. Make a reservation. Arrive early and make sure your table is ready. Ask to be seated. Choose the "power seat," which enables you to see everything that is going on in the room but restricts your lunch partner's view to you.

I realized how important this is when it happened to me by accident. I was lunching with a producer at MGM. He was being particularly helpful, offering a constructive critique of a film musical project I'd spent a year writing. I felt I needed all the help I could get. As the producer talked, I noticed out of the corner of my eye that Bo Derek was sitting at the next table. Luckily my producer didn't see her, because I was strategically placed in the "power" seat. The producer kept on about my project and I wrote down everything he said. When our lunch was over (I had great notes, just as I hoped I would), the producer stood up, saw Bo, and that was the ball game. I didn't exist anymore. Neither did my screenplay. He was totally distracted and couldn't put a sentence together. So although the location of my seat that particular day was just a lucky accident, from that time forward, I've always tried to ensure myself the power seat in any lunch or dinner meeting to avoid wasting it on distractions—Bo or otherwise.

After your guest arrives, ask him what he's going to order and request the same thing. More mirroring. If he wants a pizza with everything on it and you order a watercress salad, it'll make him feel like a slob. So whatever he's having, you're having, even if you hate it. Keep the lunch social. Ask him about himself. He probably has some great stories. Everybody does. I'm sure he'll be flattered by your interest in his business, nobody cares much about him—just what he can do for them. So this is a nice bonding time for the two of you.

Even though he may have an expense account and can write off the lunch, don't let him. You take care of the check. The one who pays the bill has the power. You're this close to getting it—go the rest of the way and grab it.

Assuming a publisher likes one of your songs and wants to publish it, you should know how to proceed. First, never negotiate your own deals. Writers are too close to their work to be objective about its value.

Have a music attorney act on your behalf. (I'm sure if Little Richard had it to do over again, he'd certainly hire a lawyer to represent his publishing contract.)

The first thing attorney Jay Cooper told me when he negotiated my first staff-writing deal was that nothing is standard. Publishers might tell you they're giving you a standard contract so you'll sign it quickly, but everything is negotiable—including the term of the agreement, which could be from six months to forever, and the royalty rate paid on sheet music, which ranges from nine cents to a quarter per copy sold. For writers who record their own material, however, record companies pay sales royalties, known as "mechanical royalties," at a reduced rate. The current mechanical royalty rate in North America for record sales is uniform, with the writers and publishers sharing 9.10 cents per copy. It varies from Web site to Web site. Publishing agreements can get complicated, so I strongly recommend you invest in a good attorney who will explain your contract to you. In addition to being able to negotiate from an objective position (because he didn't write the song, he's just representing the writer), a good attorney can get you a better deal simply because of his reputation. If Ross T. Schwartz or some other top music attorney tells a publisher he's representing you, the publisher will automatically have more respect for you and the value of your work than if a personal-injury lawyer from Des Moines calls him on your behalf.

The writer(s) and publisher of a song are partners. Each gets 50 percent of the royalties. Whether there are three or thirty writers on a song, they all share 50 percent of the income, while the publisher still gets his half. The publisher is like your agent. He represents you and the song. His job is to get your material to an artist who will record it and make you all a lot of money. Therefore, a good publisher must know who's looking for songs, which artists sell the most records, and how to make the most money in the short run—and the long run, too. A song that is a hit this year can currently earn its writer and publisher $250,000 a week, every week it's number one, and $250,000 a year every year after that for the writer's whole life plus seventy years.

A good publisher will constantly explore new ways for your songs to make money. He'll find new artists to re-record old songs. He'll get your songs in movies and on T.V. He'll arrange licensing agreements to use your hit song for a commercial. A good example is "Through the Years," a hit for Kenny Rogers that was used for a Volvo commercial. "Unforgettable" was a hit in the forties and was recently heard in a doughnut commercial. The licensing fees these songs command are astronomical. A good publisher will make sure your songs are constantly re-marketed to produce as much income as possible.

Sometimes a publisher will give you a small advance against future royalties. This could range from $100 to as much as $10,000, depending on the song and the track record of the writers. I'd always have your lawyer request an advance because the publisher will rarely, if ever, volunteer one. Also, be sure you're clear on the duration of the contract. According to the copyright law, the period for which you receive royalties on a song is the duration of the life of the writer plus seventy years. But you have to negotiate up front how long the publisher gets to keep his publishing share of your song.

Try to get a reversion clause in your contract. This means that if after a specified length of time the song hasn't been recorded, it will revert back to you. Publishers are often reluctant to include reversion clauses because it can take a long time to get a song recorded and *released*. An artist might cut twenty songs for an album but only need ten. If your song turns out to be one of the ten that didn't make it to the album, there is a chance the song might come out on the next album. And that could be a year away or longer. Artists can be dropped from their record labels. Maybe their new one wants to start over with fresh material, cut by another producer. In that case, they wouldn't want the songs left over from the early albums and "in the can." But sometimes there's a little gem of a song that sits quietly in the drawer and is suddenly released as a single because tastes change and so do song styles. That happened to Steve Dorff and me with "Let Me Love You Once Before You Go." Our song was originally recorded on a Barbara Fairchild album that was never released. Two years later, Columbia decided to release the album with our song as the single. It was a big hit. So you never know what can happen down the road. That's why publishers are reluctant to include reversion clauses. If my publisher had allowed "Let Me Love You Once Before You Go" revert back to Steve and me, he'd have done all the work of getting the song recorded for nothing. He'd have lost out because of the two-year time lapse. Publishers can only pitch songs to artists and producers. They can't control the *release* of albums. That's their argument against reversion clauses.

I always ask for one, however, and the following story illustrates why. Early in my career, when I hadn't had any meaningful records yet and nobody knew who I was, I wrote a song that was published by a major music publisher. Since they wouldn't give me an advance, they gave me a one-year reversion clause instead. If they wanted to keep the song beyond that year, they agreed in our contract to pay me $150. Although they pitched the song everywhere, when the year was up, nobody had recorded it. So I asked the president of the company if he was still interested in keeping the song. He was. I asked him when I could expect my $150 pick-up payment. He said that while the company put the clause in my contract, they didn't really *do* that anymore and didn't want to pay me. I was anxious for him to have the song if he felt he could get it cut, but at the same time, we had a deal. I said if he didn't want to pay me, he'd have to return the song. At that time, $150 was a windfall for me. But the president told me clearly that he didn't want to "throw good money after bad," and gave me back my song.

Nine months later, I signed a staff-writing deal with Almo Music and became a salaried employee in exchange for giving them the publishing rights to all the songs I wrote during a one-year period. Since the song in question had reverted back to me at the end of its deal at the other publishing company, I assigned the copyright to Almo Music, my new publisher, and rewrote it. It got cut right away. A year later, my song "Silver Wings and Golden Rings" won an ASCAP Country Music Award for being one of the most performed songs of the year. What made that success even sweeter was at the awards banquet, I was seated next to the man from the first publishing company who had originally told me the song wasn't worth $150. That night he graciously toasted me and confessed he should never have let the song go. But that reversion clause made my career. Be sure you don't leave any songs behind if you can help it.

As in any business, music publishers are comfortable doing business with people they know. The most successful songwriters I've met are fantastic schmoozers. Just as most of the deals in the Fortune 500 community are made on the golf course, many of the most successful music publishing and record deals are also made there, or on the tennis court, in the steam room, or on the Little League diamond. It may seem callous and calculating, but if I were in Nashville trying to break in, I can assure you that I would be attending charity events to which I knew the publishers, A & R people, and the record company executives were passionate contributors. I'd be, as we say, "in their face," so they'd get used to seeing me. When it came time to do business, I wouldn't be a stranger. People hate doing business with strangers. This is not reinventing the wheel. This is the way business is done in every sector of the American economy, and it's no different in the music business.

While songwriters tend to think that music publishers who reject them are the enemy, the truth is music publishers want the very same things that songwriters do, and that is great songs they can pitch and get recorded. It must be terribly frustrating for publishers to keep having to say no. They must walk around with an awful lot of guilt. They are sensitive people, and they want to say yes, but they know what they have to deal with on the other side of the next desk, and the next. They also have to keep their jobs. Nobody wants to pitch songs that are almost there but not hits yet, because no music publisher wants to be unemployed. So I try to make it okay for somebody to say no to me. Even though I feel stabbed in the heart, and should call an ambulance, somehow I find it in myself to say, "Hey, we're on the same team, we want the same things, we'll try again soon."

Remember, the music business is a business. Your songs are the currency of that business. Give them what they want.

♪ WHAT DOES PUBLISHING REALLY MEAN IN THE MUSIC BUSINESS?

It's important to know that when a song is published, the publisher will present you with a contract, which you will first, of course, have your music attorney review, not some online paralegal who handles dog bites in The Outer Hebrides. In the book business, when a book is published, you get a book. But when a song is published, you get a contract, and it's only *after* the song is a hit that sheet music is actually printed. While getting a song published is an important step in a songwriting career, it's not the final one. The goal is getting the song *recorded and released*.

I know what it's like to be new, believe me, and to want more than anything else to have my songs published and recorded. That first yes is so important. But it's also critical to get the yes from a music publisher who's really a music publisher. Anybody can be one. You simply register a name with ASCAP, BMI, or SESAC. But the real question is what has that publishing company achieved? Songwriters have to ask the tough questions, tough questions to which they don't necessarily get answers they like. If you suddenly receive a contract in the mail, before you sign it, ask the publisher, "What songs do you have on the charts right now? What songs have you had on the charts in the past?" Verify all of that before you sign anything. As artists, we are so vulnerable and needy of other people's approval that we forget the due diligence with our business affairs and often suffer as a result of that. So ask the tough questions and ask them nicely. I might say, for example, "Forgive me, I'm new to the music business and I am not familiar with your work. Could you tell me some of the hits your company has published and some of the artists who've recorded them?" Verify everything you're told. Again, I know how important it is for you to have a song published to get the ball rolling, but there's no point in signing up with a shark.

There seem to be plenty of people these days who are desperate to publish your songs as long as you pay them to do that, a course of action as valuable as setting fire to the money you would spend to do what they propose. A legitimate publisher will present you with a contract that will pass the scrutiny of your entertainment lawyer. When the song or songs that you've had published by that publisher earn royalties, *he* sends *you* money. You don't send it to him. I tell all my clients that may not be what they want to hear, but it is the truth.

Here is another very important point that new writers need to know. Music publishers are not interested in pieces of songs. They don't want lyrics only, and they don't want music only. They want to hear finished songs. You might think that's a crisis if you write lyrics only or melodies only, but it doesn't have to be. As a consultant, I have been very, very lucky matching lyricists, composers, and singers. So if you write part of a song and want to find the rest of it, give me a call, or go to my Web site, songmd.com, and right there under "Molly's Store" you'll see exactly how to set up a consultation with me. Then I can review your work and help you find the right collaborators. *For legal reasons, anything that arrives in my office without my consulting fee enclosed, must, regrettably, be deleted immediately. Thank you for respecting the professional parameters of my consultancy.*

♪ IN THEIR FACE

I suggest to all my clients that they go to as many industry events as possible. Everybody they want to know and do business with is there. The best event, by far, is the Grammys, held in February each year. I recommend you join the National Academy of Recording Arts and Sciences, thereby being eligible to buy tickets to that gala. While it would be fun just to go and sit up in the rafters, I urge you to save up and get really good seats, which would allow you to attend the After Party, where everybody who was nominated and everybody who won is present, along with their agents, managers, dog therapists, past-life cuticle removers, and spiritual advisers/bookies. I suggest that instead of saying, "Hi, my name is Molly Leikin. I'm a songwriter and I'd like to send you a tune, or I'd like to send you my CD," I would use that evening to congratulate everybody, especially the people who are not in the limelight, for the good job they've done. Nobody really knows the faces of music publishers, other than the people in the music business, so if you walked up to the president of Warner/Chappell and said, "I'm really proud of you. Congratulations on your success. It's a great record. You've got great ears, and good for you," you'd be remembered. Ask for a business card, even trade business cards, and then the very next day, send everyone you met the night before a personal note, not an e-mail, a hand-written, personal note. Write something like, "Congratulations. I'm proud of you. It's a well-earned honor." Then, a week later, call and say, "When your desk is clear, I'd love to talk to you about an exciting, new project that we can do together." Sounds cocky and arrogant, yes. But somebody might bite.

See, everybody congratulates the stars, but in a music publishing company, the only thing anybody usually hears is what he's done wrong. So this would be a real change of pace and is something that would definitely attract the recipient's attention. They don't want to hear, "I've been sleeping with my eleven orphaned children in a stolen car, and my unemployment ran out at the same time my husband ran off with his brother-in-law's lyricist's hypnotist." I would confine my comments to: "I know we're going to make money and history together." The point is to make your approach from a position of power rather than need. And if you don't feel you have any power, then pump yourself up with positive affirmations about your work so you do.

♪ COURAGE

When music publishers turn us down, we think they are the enemy, but they're not. They need us, and we need them. Without our new music, where would they be? Judy Harris, of Judy Harris Music in Nashville, who published the smash hit "Tequila Makes Her Clothes Fall Off," said, "I encourage artists and writers alike to perform and write the best song, remembering at the same time that they don't have to have lived that song personally, it's just the best song they can find or write." David Ross, of Music Row Publications, says, "You write because you love to write, you need to write. It's not about the money. But if you do your job correctly, you start getting hits."

And Bruce Broughton, who is on the ASCAP board, said, "As for encouraging new artists, I would suggest two practical things: in addition to continue working hard at your craft and improving your creative ability, try to find your voice. Even as styles change around you, get to know your market and try to develop a very thick skin."

The main thing is to do your art no matter what. Nobody has the right to shut you down. You know you've got something special to contribute to the literature of music. And I can't wait to hear it.

10

Making Money in the Meantime

Although the "struggling artist" has been romanticized in movies and books, it's no fun being poor. I was. I don't recommend it. Not having income puts tremendous pressure on you to make money quickly with your writing. That isn't fair to you. You should be writing songs to express yourself, to share your feelings with the world. Don't put the demand of financial survival on your songwriting too early or it could squash your chances forever. I don't know any great songwriter who has lasted and writes just for the money.

While the ultimate goal for most songwriters is a smash hit that's downloaded 24/7 all over the Web, there are ways of earning substantial income using songwriting skills while aiming at less competitive and more lucrative short-run markets.

The first thing you must know is never to take no for an answer. Ever. Write that a hundred times a day and repeat it to yourself while you're soliciting work. If somebody turns you down, learn why, change your pitch a little, and go back again with a new angle. Success is contagious. You'll see how people who've dismissed you as a hack suddenly love you when you've been successful elsewhere.

♪ WARNING

You never sell your songs. Never. You have them *published.* When that occurs, you receive 50 percent of the income from them. Even though a publisher may give you a cash advance against future royalties from the song, you still have not *sold* the publisher your work. You will always receive the writer's share of the income derived from that song. Even if someone offers you a million dollars to buy your song outright, never do it. If you have a hit this year, it could earn you $250,000 per year every year for the rest of your life, and make the same amount for your estate for another seventy years after your death. So songs are *not* for sale. Only the publishing rights are. Unfortunately, there are shysters out there who prey on inexperience in the music business. Let me give you an example. In the fifties, Little Richard was just a naive kid from the backwoods when an unscrupulous weasel came along, had him sign on the dotted line, and gave him $10,000—more than the young singer/songwriter could possibly imagine having in three lifetimes. What Little Richard didn't realize until later was that because he was so hungry for success and because $10,000 seemed like such a windfall to him at the time, he didn't read the contract carefully or have it reviewed by a reputable attorney. That $10,000 was all the income Little Richard ever saw from those copyrights. He should have received royalties for all his hits—"Long Tall Sally," "Slippin' and Slidin'," "Lucille," "Rip It Up," "Ready Teddy," "Tutti-Frutti," "Good Golly Miss Molly"—plus many other songs that he wrote and recorded. Now he is suing his publisher for $50,000,000. *So never sell your songs.*

You should also *never give any record company money to record your songs.* There are vanity companies run by song sharks stashed away in smarmy places across the country. These people know how hard it is for a writer or artist to make a deal through normal music-business channels. They promise to record and release your songs and maybe even get them played two or three times on a local station. They charge you from $500 to $10,000 to make a record and will even send you sample copies with your picture on them. But nothing ever comes of this. They are simply preying on your ego and counting on your impatience. *They are in business to rip you off.* Sure, you get your song or your album recorded, but by musicians who crank out fifty songs a day, making them all sound alike. These companies never have national distribution or legitimate connections with meaningful radio stations. A legitimate record company pays you royalties. *So never send anybody money to publish your songs. Ever.*

♪ JINGLES

While you're learning the business of music and are slowly building credibility and contacts, write jingles. Try a local store or business. Offer to write a jingle for free. You need the credit and the reputation of being able to deliver. Good news travels fast. Figure you'll get paid for the next gig. From there you could move up to a national account and get residuals. That's fine. We'll take it. Your jingle could play for years. Sometimes commercials become hits—like "We've Only Just Begun" and more recently "The Pride Is Back." That's okay. We'll take that, too. Any success on this level will give you the luxury of having time to write the songs you really want to write.

Most jingle writers have a "reel" containing samples of their work. You'll need one, too. If you don't have one, write a couple of jingles to showcase yourself. Take nationally advertised products like Coca-Cola, Ford, and McDonald's and write something new for each account. Produce a professional-sounding demo and use it as a calling card for your first jingle gig. That shows a lot of moxie. People in that business respect it. Play the game by their rules.

Most developing writers have been rejected so often and are so anxious to have their work recognized that when someone does want their material, they are eager to give it away. In the case of jingles, most advertisers will want to offer you a "buy-out" deal, for which they'd pay you a flat fee for the use of your song and they'd own it from then on. You wouldn't receive any further royalties, even if it ran on the air for fifteen years. Remember the commercial for cereal, the one in which "Mikey liked it"? I believe it was on the air for sixteen years. Imagine how awful you'd feel if you'd signed a buy-out deal on that one. So if someone wants to buy you out, what you have to do is politely turn that down, and suggest instead that you'll allow them to *use* or license the song for a year for a specified amount of money. If they want to use it for succeeding years, they'll have to pay you another lump sum at the beginning of each new term. That protects both of you. The jingle company doesn't have to put out a huge amount of money in the short run, and you will have some income protection for the future. Plus— and this is a big plus—when your jingles are performed, you should receive what is known as "small performances" on them. Here's how that works.

Whenever a song is performed for profit, it earns money. The performing rights societies, ASCAP, BMI, and SESAC, constantly survey radio stations, TV stations, cable stations, and the Web for all pieces of music played on the air. Each radio and TV station has to purchase an annual license to air copyrighted material, and songwriters are paid quarterly. In order to determine which songs are played during that year, the performing rights societies survey the stations for all performances for profit. Jingles are included in this category, but are paid at a much smaller royalty rate than regular songs. If you have a jingle that's played a lot, however, those small pert performances can add up. Always include them when negotiating a contract for a jingle. They are payable to both the writer and the publisher of the song, so the sums we're discussing here are considerable. Whatever you do, don't let some fast-talking guy who works out of the trunk of his stolen car schmooze you out of your small performances. If you don't get them, he will, under the guise of being the publisher. Let him be publisher, but don't let him collect your small performance royalties as a writer, too.

Developing writers may argue with me by saying that you have to let one go to get something else. But look at it this way. What if the stars have determined you will have this one jingle and it'll be your only source of income for the next twenty years until you have that long-awaited smash? Then how stupid and abused will you feel if you didn't demand the small performances that are legally yours? They aren't paid by the jingle company, but by the radio station. So demand them. And get them.

♪ NO UNION PROTECTION

What's always been interesting to me is that when commercials are performed, the arranger automatically gets royalties. So does every singer and musician. But there is no songwriters' or jingle writers' union, so it's still dog-eat-dog out there. I'm hoping that by reading this chapter and referring to it again and again, you will not be robbed of royalties and income that is rightfully yours.

♪ CUSTOM-TAILORED TUNES

Write personalized limericks or sonnets and set them to music for weddings, birthdays, anniversaries, graduations, Mother's Day, Father's Day, Valentine's Day, and Christmas. Gain a reputation for being clever, accommodating, getting the job done on time, and pleasing the client. That will help you in your other pursuits, because while you're doing this alternative line of work only until you can write songs full-time, so are most of the people you come in contact with along the way. You never know whether the receptionist at the Gorilla Company will become president of Sony/BMG someday. People are more apt to do business with someone they already know and with whom they've had success in the past. Move up together. Make that your motto.

♪ COPYWRITING

If you're a lyricist and can't write music, be a copywriter. That uses related skills. Selling a product and selling a song are the same. The tag lines used in advertising are like song titles—short and snappy. You'll be earning money as a writer, not a waiter, and you'll be working with creative people. Who knows? Maybe the agency employing you will need a jingle at some point.

That happened to a copywriter on the Kodak account. His company hired Roger Nichols, composer of "We've Only Just Begun" and ''I Won't Last a Day Without You," to write a melody for a new Kodak campaign. The copywriter, who to the best of my knowledge had never had a hit song before, was there at the right time and did the lyric for "Good Morning Yesterday," which turned into a commercial and later a smash hit for Paul Anka.

♪ TEACH

If you're more musically than lyrically oriented, teach music: guitar, piano, or voice. You'll be earning a living, working "in the business," and you never know who will walk through your door.

♪ HIRE A LAWYER

Most creative people are terrible negotiators. They can't separate themselves from the product they're selling. I would strongly recommend you always have someone else do your deal-making for you, just as you would when negotiating a publishing contract.

Never trust verbal agreements. Always get it in writing. If a guy won't sign an agreement, he won't pay you, either. So always, always insist on a contract and hire an entertainment lawyer to handle it for you, not someone who writes up time-share contracts in suburban Tibet.

While you're exploring alternative sources of income within the writing and music fields, you're sharpening your writing skills. You're learning to tailor your songs to specific requirements, which is what you must do when writing for a particular artist. Who knows when you'll bump into someone during your scuffling days who wants a real song? If you're used to writing on assignment, you'll be ready for anything and will do a terrific job. Satisfied customers will come back to you for more. What you're doing here is taking charge of your life, creating cash flow, and gaining confidence as a writer. That last item, confidence, is the most important ingredient you have for sale, both to yourself and to prospective customers.

11

Seasons

It's essential for all songwriters to remember that even the most successful of their heroes and colleagues have suffered enormous defeats, setbacks, and failures. But they bounced back.

I've had publishers throw me out of their offices, tossing my demos after me and yelling, "Gimme somethin' I can dance to." And just a few months later, those same songs got standing ovations at Carnegie Hall. So who's right? The insensitive publisher or the appreciative audience in New York?

Don't be intimidated by rock stars' youthful ages. Many are grandparents.

All artists suffer from rejection. Each of us feels stabbed at the time and inevitably retreats to a safe place under the bed, or the truck, until we work through the pain, can remember who we are and that there is value in what we've done. Our work might just be positioned in the wrong segment of the marketplace for the moment.

All my favorite artists—painters, dancers, sculptors, composers—have suffered highs and lows in their careers, and it is very gratifying to know they made it through and created their best work at the end of that long black tunnel of nothing. I have a million rejection stories of my own. The best one, with the happiest ending so far, has to do with a song called "I Hear Your Heart."

I was collaborating with a singer/songwriter. We had written two sensational songs together, and I gave her lyric three, thinking she'd love it. Instead I got a nasty e-mail, saying, "That's the worst thing I've ever seen. I couldn't possibly sing it. Your lyric is demeaning. I'll go blind if I have to see those words again. Can't possibly work with you anymore. I'm outta here."

Oh?

I took that for a no.

As much as I was disappointed, I knew my lyric was especially good, and I figured someday I'd have a use for it, although I had no idea how far out that someday might be. So I put the words aside, sighed for a couple of days, and went on with the rest of my life.

Two years later, I was invited to participate in a collaboration with some European tunesmiths. Our agreement was to write eight songs together. They'd do the melodies, and I'd do the words. Fine. We completed seven good songs, but came up empty on the eighth. That's when I suggested that I write the lyric first and have them write the tune later, promising to help with the rhythm, because I knew English was not their first language. And out of the drawer comes "I Hear Your Heart." But when I sent it to the Europeans, their reaction was, "We don't get it." Swell. However, we still needed the eighth song. They kept sending melodies that just didn't sing to me, I sent six more lyrics they rejected and finally re-submitted "I Hear Your Heart," which they turned down again. My lyrics seemed to be doing more damage to international relations than Al-Qaeda. At one point, I expected the CIA at my door to arrest me for subversive activities.

Meanwhile, I took a lot of yoga classes and hiked all the trails in the Santa Ynez mountains, hoping for a solution that was fair and equitable for all of us.

Cut to a homeless kid sleeping on the couch of my European composer's office. He refused to leave until the composer listened to his CD. God bless this young man, who fished my discarded lyric out of the trash, because a few weeks later, my assistant opened up the e-mail and found an MP3 with that kid singing a cappella, and the song was fantastic! The young man was in a group called Cosmos, and they had some kind of a label deal in the Balkans, of all places, and the next thing I know, I'm getting phone calls in the middle of the night from people with thick Slavic accents, saying that our song "I Hear Your Heart" was in the finals of *Eurovision*. The finals of *what*? At the time I didn't know what *Eurovision* was, but gleefully and triumphantly discovered that it's like *American Idol*, but instead of being just for one country, it was for forty-two. According to my ASCAP checks, being finalists is a very big deal. So all those previous nos that I suffered through turned

into a great big yes. I had another huge hit and another season in the
sun.

All of my colleagues—*your* colleagues—have stories like these. The
bottom line is persistence. If you don't give up, your time will come. A
writer's job is to write. If you write well and pursue originality and
perfection, the world will know your work. But until then, you must
feel in your soul that you've got the greatness and the magic to go the
distance. No gold record, no Grammy can give you that. You have to
give it to yourself. Every day. All day. For the rest of your life.

People get hot and cold. When you get hot, it's because you created
the heat. When you're cold, don't fall into the trap of thinking somebody took something away from you. I have colleagues who've gone
from a Mercedes to a skateboard and back to a Mercedes again. Some
are hitchhiking in Gucci shoes. We don't live in straight lines. We
zigzag. Andy Warhol claimed we each get fifteen minutes in the spotlight.
While I disagree with his timetable, I do concur that we don't get lucky
and stay hot forever. It's a roller coaster called "the music business." If
you want to ride along with us, buy your ticket and be prepared. Just
remember when you're in a slump, it is only temporary. If George
Burns and Tina Turner can come back, so can you.

Write well. Surprise me. Dazzle me. I'm counting on it. You are the
future of music. The world needs your songs. Please—don't let us down.

12
Music on
the Internet

My world has changed dramatically since I wrote the first edition of this book. (This is the fifth edition.) I left What's-His Name-with-the-Silver-Blue-Eyes, bought Pro Tools, and finally have a backhand plus a serve in my tennis game. After being left for dead for twenty-four years at A&M, my song "Tangled Up in Tears," co-written with Albert Hammond, went double platinum with a gypsy artist named Azucar Moreno.

I sold my townhouse to Robert Redford, (yes, *the* Robert Redford), bought a home on a quiet street that is—knock wood—Doberman-free, and have watched with pride as more and more of my clients reach the charts. But by far, the most startling and creative changes in my life, and everyone else's, has been the rise of the Internet.

In the early '90s, I'd heard about the World Wide Web, but being so non-technical that I expected the Nobel Prize for simply turning on a light switch without popping the bulb, I thought the information superhighway was just for financial portfolios and pornography, not necessarily in that order. So when my childhood friend Jacqueline Paradis Lamont, whom I hadn't seen in twenty-five years, visited me in La Jolla, California, and suggested that I get a Web page and go online, I couldn't imagine why. Me? Use a computer? On the Internet?

Well, Jaci made a very valuable suggestion. I've had a Web site since 1994. It's called Songwriting Consultants, Ltd., and the address is: www.songmd.com. Every day, hundreds of songwriters, singers, and bands from all over the world contact me, asking for my professional help in furthering their dreams and careers. It's very exciting to work with talented writers and artists of varied and interesting backgrounds.

I've learned so much of their different cultures and look forward one day to meeting them all face to face, when I take a year off again to see the world.

As much experience as I've had with the Internet, when I decided to write this chapter, I called my friend Randy Grimmett at ASCAP's West Coast office in Los Angeles to see who their "Web guy" was. Randy said it was Ron Sobel, vice president of membership and creative affairs. Ron, who headed the West Coast office, was very generous in spending time with me to make sure all of my information was current.

Here are some major reasons for songwriters/bands/musicians to use the Internet:

1. You can find every company you'd like to work with, and everybody in that company, by doing just a few minutes' research using a search engine, like Google or Yahoo!

2. People who will never take phone calls or answer "snail mail" are more likely to answer e-mail.

3. While it's easy to lose touch with people you don't see frequently, it's very simple to send a friendly e-mail every month or so, which keeps you "in their face," which is where you have to be in our business. Period. But don't abuse this. Too much e-mail is a real turn-off.

4. Even if you live in West of Nowhere, Nebraska, or East of Everything, Maine, you can still create a community of writers and a support "Internetwork" for your songs through the friends you find online. More than anything, an artist needs a support group. That is often hard to find in a town where everyone else is a steel-worker or a shepherd.

5. By creating a Web site of your own, you have a great "calling card"—a way of introducing yourself and your music to the world. People who won't necessarily take your calls or the time to listen to a stranger's CD may get curious and stop by to listen for a minute. If what you present is professional and polished, you might get lucky. However, after having a Web site all these years, I have to caution you that pushing too hard is very alienating, whether it's in person or online. As a case in point, I get hundreds of e-mails a day, asking me to visit Web sites and listen to songs

and to give feedback on my dime. When I say I don't do business that way, suddenly I'm the bad guy. Truthfully, there is a fine line between being persistent and being a pest. Persistent and clever might catch someone's attention. But persistent and annoying will get you deleted immediately. Ask my assistant.

6. One of the most positive features of the Internet is the opportunity it gives you to create an e-mail list—and send press releases to everyone on it. In this quick and inexpensive way, you can tell the world in general, and the music industry in particular, about your new projects and triumphs.

7. If there was someone you used to do business with, say at S&M Music Publishing in the '90s, and he/she isn't there anymore, assuming he/she is not in prison, it could be quite easy to find that person again by using a search engine. Ideally your contact has moved to another music publishing company and can resume a positive business relationship with you there. So the Internet is a great detective tool.

♪ COPYRIGHT

Too many writers get frustrated by anonymity and want to give their music away just to get it heard. But there's a way to use the Internet intelligently, getting the exposure you want without doing anything silly or stupid and end up giving away the store.

Before sending a song to anyone, whether it's a lyric, a melody, a track, a demo, or a finished master, via e-mail, snail mail, on CD, or by carrier pigeon, a smart writer will always make sure that work is copyrighted. I don't mean sending a registered letter to yourself. I mean filing an official copyright notice. On the Internet, it is still impossible to prove access, and therefore impossible to tell who's heard your work. I urge you to copyright everything you post online or send, solicited or otherwise, to anyone—even your momma. I won't accept a song for a consultation that does not bear the copyright symbol (©) plus your name and the year the song was written, and I urge you to make sure each song you write has that symbol on it before sending it to anyone. In addition, it would be worth your while to seek the advice of a competent music attorney—not someone who does real estate in

Red Deer, Alberta—but an experienced music lawyer. That way, you can make sure your work is protected. Otherwise, if you post your music online or send it by e-mail it to someone, I feel you're inviting disaster.

Another important consideration is to make sure your work is protected by an international copyright. In some countries, a copyright is just good for that territory. But since most of us think globally these days, an international copyright is recommended. Since the law is different in each country, I urge you to check it in your jurisdiction, to make sure your work has an international copyright, not just a local one.

The Internet produces incredible challenges and opportunities. Here are the three main ways it can help a developing writer:

1. It is a medium, like radio, with all of the same benefits.
2. It is a marketplace. E-commerce is booming.
3. It is a tool and a resource to provide information, answers, and links.

Ron Sobel felt there are a lot of reasons for a writer to take advantage of the opportunities on the Internet: If you are an emerging writer who lives in Boise, Idaho, and has absolutely no connections in the major music cities like Los Angeles, Nashville, Miami, London, or New York, after consulting with a good music attorney, you may decide that putting a song or two online might be a good marketing tool to generate interest in your work.

As of this writing, there is incredible traffic and activity among bands and writers online. Hundreds of thousands of writers, who had no chance of connecting from home with the power players in our industry before the rise of the Internet, now have a shot. If I had a major record label, I'd be sure to have some hot, young A & R people searching the Internet for new acts and new writers. The major labels are starting to "get it."

True, lots of songs are weak and undeveloped—and their writers should make a point of learning the craft of songwriting *before* sending out tunes to anybody. That's a given. Attempting to market something in an amateur form is a waste of time in the real world, as well as in the virtual one. Truthfully, it would be more productive to set fire to hundred-dollar bills.

But assuming you've done your homework, studied songwriting, and learned the craft of our art, many of the Web sites that are in the business of showcasing music "filter" or critique it for publishers and A & R people. So everything is prescreened, thereby not wasting anyone's valuable time. Assuming you've polished your work and have run it by a professional or two (not your uncle Bubba or your groupie) and have gotten the go-ahead that it is ready to realistically compete in the marketplace, here are some showcase sites:

iTunes
CD baby
MySpace.com

Ron Sobel felt these Web sites create astounding opportunities for artists in remote areas to gain yet another avenue of access to the existing ones. "There aren't a lot of music publishers taking calls from Des Moines, but writers can post their songs on the Internet and get reviews on a hundred sites. Even if sixty to seventy thousand writers send in their music for consideration, the cream still rises to the top." (All the more reason to make sure your work is ready for the real world and the marketplace *before* sending it anywhere, don't you agree?)

I asked Ron how writers are being compensated for their music being played on the Internet. "ASCAP, BMI, and SESAC are all licensing Web sites. Each year since 1997, the number of licensed sites has tripled. Do the math. Think where that will put us in five years."

Here's where the money comes from: if someone downloads your CD from the Internet and pays you for it, there may be a performance royalty and a mechanical royalty paid to the writer, if the song shows up in a survey. There is also a lot of money to be made on a local basis. Writers in Anchorage, Alaska, or on the Mexican border no longer have to pack up and move to a music center. "Writers in Dodge aren't doomed for dead-ends anymore," Ron said. "They can make a nice living in their local markets, thanks, in the most part, to the Internet . . . . You still have to shake hands, do lunch, play golf, and perform live. Absolutely. But using the Internet is a good way to get started." So if you don't happen to live in Los Angeles, New York City, or Nashville, that's okay. Stay where you are. But ASCAP, BMI, and

SESAC send their people all over the country looking for new talent. Many new acts and producers have been discovered and promoted off the World Wide Web.

"We're in day one of the Internet," Ron said. "Don't be intimidated, be educated. It's *one* of the things you do, it's not *all* you do." So if you don't have a mainstream deal with a label or publisher, you can still be in the music business locally and make a nice living. You'll be a big fish in a small pond, but there will be water in that pond. You can sell your CDs yourself, and instead of making a 10 percent royalty as you would with a major label, you will get 100 percent. Say you sell your CDs for $10.00 or $15.00 each. Do the math. If you sell 5,000, that's a living; whereas if you sell 50,000 CDs on a major label, you are considered a total failure by the bean counters, and will probably be dropped immediately, if not sooner.

"Be advised that the Internet doesn't blow away the traditional options, it enhances them," Sobel said.

Back in the traditional music business, professionals are using the Internet in incredible ways. Tracks are cut in one city and e-mailed to another for vocals. Records are made with drummers in Holland, ukulele players in Carpinteria, producers in London, and mixers on the moon.

Here are Ron's top-five reasons for using the Internet in our business:

1. It allows for the creative community to receive new revenue streams from advertising, subscriptions, and stock and venture capital options.
2. E-mail addresses have become the single most valuable piece of revenue that an emerging writer can get. It gives a writer/band a direct connection with a potential fan. In the past, you went to a record store, bought a CD, and left. But if someone likes your work on the Internet, you have a way to get in touch with fans and really communicate. You can also expand your market. So the Internet helps you create a following as an artist.
3. The enlightened professionals in the music business are going to really take advantage of the power of the Internet. One Web label is atomicpop.com. To locate others that will inevitably change after the publication of this book, please type "online record labels" in your search engine.

4. The Internet gives you the option of making and marketing your own songs, and using an Internet distributor. The top one is CD Baby.

5. You can have niche marketing and small-market success without having to go the traditional route of required radio airplay before you can sell yourself and your CDs. You can have a regional career by selling 1,000, 2,000, or 5,000 CDs, perform locally, and make a very good living. Make no mistake about it, you still need great songs, and they still require that you learn the craft of songwriting first before marketing them anywhere in the world.

Ron felt, as I do, that a new writer should be mindful of the challenges and pitfalls of the Internet. But in his opinion, the opportunities far outweigh the problems.

So if you're not online, have a look some rainy Sunday afternoon and see what's happening music-wise on the World Wide Web. If you're already there, I hope you check, as my Webmaster does every day, to see what's new. As quickly as things happen in this world, many of the companies and business activities on the Internet could change completely by sundown. (I asked my editor if I could wait until the very last millisecond to publish this chapter, to make sure I was as current as possible with this information.) As new developments arise online, I'll bring them to you. So stop by my Web site, songmd.com, and say hello, read my bi-weekly column, and find out the latest innovations and trends in the music business. I'll be waiting for you with a cup of hot peppermint tea, an open ear, and a good joke.

Write well. I'm rooting for you.

♪ ♪ ♪

This chapter is dedicated to the memory of Ron Anton.
No matter what was or wasn't happening in my career,
Ron always made me feel proud to hold a pencil.
I miss him.

13

Interview with Melissa Etheridge

Melissa Etheridge grew up in Leavenworth, Kansas, where the main industries were the army base and the prison. Her first gigs were singing for inmates. "Nobody else liked me, but the prisoners sure did," Melissa chuckled. After high school, she enrolled at the Berklee College of Music in Boston, got a part-time job as a security guard, and sang in the Park St. subway station for extra money. After a few weeks at Berklee, Melissa was dissatisfied with the curriculum and left school, but continued to sing in the subway station. She was able to make enough money from tips in her guitar case to squeak by. That gave her a lot of courage to keep singing.

"I might have been able to build up a following in Boston, but people would only listen to me until their trains left, so you couldn't exactly say I had a captive audience the way I did singing in the prisons." From there, she went back home to Kansas, gigging in hotels, where she had to perform other people's songs. "It was an incredible learning experience as a songwriter. When you think on *other* people's songs that have been hits and you start to realize, what is successful, what do people like? Well, this is a song everybody sings on the chorus. Why? Why does everyone like that chorus? This is a song everyone is comfortable to buy. Why? Why is it successful? And I learned all about songwriting, and I sang everything from Neil Diamond to Paul Simon to Fleetwood Mac.

"But Kansas just wasn't for me anymore, and I went out to California. Everything was happening in Hollywood. I looked through the calendar section of the *Los Angeles Times*, trying to find places that had live music. I'd heard of the Troubadour, but that was 1982, and I go to the Troubadour and there's LA Guns and Ratts and Poisons, and these huge, heavy metal-sounding bands, and nobody wanted to have any-thing to do with a girl and a guitar. So I just couldn't find any work, and I couldn't get paid, because everybody plays for free in LA, and so it was like, uh-oh, I'm running out of money, I'm gonna have to find myself a real job."

Not able to afford her own apartment, Melissa moved onto her aunt's couch forty miles away in Long Beach, which is hardly the music capital of the world, but lots closer to Hollywood than Kansas. For five years, Melissa played her guitar in what she refers to as girl bars. "I did okay," she said. "I played in Pasadena, too, did the Women's Music Festival, and I felt, well, that's fine, I'll just be on Olivia Records and that'll be that." Then she sent her CD to Olivia Records, they said, "No thank you," and she was back playing in a bar in Pasadena.

"Every Sunday, the gals would come in after their soccer game to have some drinks and listen to me, and there was someone on their team who had a friend whose husband was in artist management." They all loved Melissa and wanted to get their girlfriend to bring in her husband. Well, the wife came by, and she was excited about Melissa's talent and convinced her husband to come in to watch her perform. After hearing one song, that was it. Bill Leopold signed her.

But it took five years of singing in the bars and singing in the clubs and getting paid next to nothing before she met Bill, who after twenty-five years is still her manager. Melissa says that Bill told her, "You know, you've got a good thing here, you're making a living. I'm not going to take you out of these bars because you have a following." But he said, "I'm gonna get you a label deal."

"And slowly, over the years," Melissa recalled, "he got everybody from the LA music scene to come out, and one by one, they all said they liked me, they loved me, but you know, I couldn't get a hit song, and they just didn't know what to do with me. Every single company came out, and every single one of them turned me down. And that lasted for five years. The bar in Long Beach was called Que Sera Sera, and as soon as I got signed to a label, it was no longer just a women's bar. Now it's a place where live bands perform. They have a big stage and it's a great music club."

Two years after Melissa met Bill Leopold, a publisher from A&M came in and signed her to be a staff writer. She was getting a weekly advance of $250, which was a windfall to her. However, the "M" from A&M, Jerry Moss, was really upset that his company was paying her all that money and she wasn't writing songs for Whitney Houston like his other staff writers. "So there was absolutely no return on his money yet," Melissa remembered. "And he was really impatient and wanted to drop me." He was a businessman, and had a business to run. "Finally, a producer from A&M knew Chris Blackwell at Island Records, and said there's this girl I want you to hear, she's singing down the street." Chris locked the car doors and drove him the forty miles through LA traffic to Long Beach, where he heard four songs and signed her. That was 1988, and Melissa finally had a deal on Island Records. "I knew this was the only thing I could do that moved my soul. This was the only dream I ever had. Plenty of times I was discouraged, and drove up to the top of Mulholland Drive and asked, when is this gonna happen? I'm not quitting, but how long do I have to wait?

"When I was a child, I would go down to the basement, and I would write sad songs, really sad songs. I would write about the old man and the children who got lost in the woods and the old man helping them out, all these incredible stories, and my girlfriends would cry. People would allow me to have my emotions through music." But Melissa was not allowed to have those feelings anywhere else. "I cultivated this emotional release and I got to put my anger in it, and the anger became rock 'n' roll. I didn't understand where things were going, and nobody understood lovers being gay, and that was rock 'n' roll. And I would still write those songs whenever I had feelings or emotions. I would sit in my bedroom and I would write those songs for me. Well, what happened is, in these bars where I was playing, I'm playing the songs I think everybody's gonna like. One of the first songs I played to the people, the ten people at the bar, I said that it was my own personal experience, and that was the first song that somebody came up and said, will you play that song that you wrote, I really like that song.

"And I started to realize that the truth resonated with people. The inspiration is from the universe; the craft shows up in the rewrite. That's where the true songwriter comes out. I'm always looking for another way to say it. After writing "I'm the Only One" and "Come to My Window," I realized I struck a chord with women who felt emotionally run over. It was cathartic for them. I had found a niche.

"Then I got out of that bad relationship I was writing about, and I fell completely in love. I am completely happy, but nothing happened with the songs I've written since I've been so happy. So I thought, maybe there's no room for me anymore in this industry, certainly not on the radio, they won't play me. And I figured that my career was over, and I'd lost my desire to create. But then again, maybe I'll just write children's songs for my kids.

"Then, next day, I was taking a shower and found the lump. I had breast cancer." During her chemotherapy, Melissa experienced an enormous spiritual awakening. She gave a phenomenal performance at the Grammys that year, blew the roof off the Staples Center, and that told her heart she was coming back to life.

And what a life! In 2000, Melissa Etheridge opened for Vice President Al Gore while he was campaigning to be president of the United States. When Melissa's fans came to see her at those gigs, she would tell them that a vote for Ralph Nader was really like a vote for the Republicans, so please vote for the Democrats. Then she introduced the crowd to Vice President Gore. Melissa and the VP had a strong friendship and a very positive connection. Al Gore believed in Melissa as much as she believed in him. He called the day after her stunning Grammy performance to congratulate her, and even came to her wedding.

Then one afternoon, when Melissa was back up on Mulholland Drive wondering what on earth to do about her career, the phone rang, and it was Al asking her to come to a slideshow he had prepared about global warming. It was being filmed, he said, and he wanted her to be in the audience. After the slideshow, Mr. Gore asked Melissa if she would please write a song for a documentary they were making of it, and she did.

But it was not an easy gig. She wrote two songs that she threw out, and was really stuck in a way that she hadn't ever been before. "One of the approaches was preachy, we should do this, we should do that, and one approach was from the vice president's point of view, and neither of them worked or clicked in my gut," Melissa admitted. Finally, her wife, Tammy, came into the office and suggested that Melissa make the song more personal, and with that point of view, the song got written very quickly. Melissa made a demo, sent it to the vice president, who called her the next day, absolutely overwhelmed, pleased, and so proud to have that song for his film. He was especially happy that Melissa included the title of the documentary, *An Inconvenient Truth,* in her lyric. The film won an Oscar, and so did Melissa for writing "I Need to Wake Up," the first time a woman had won the Oscar for Best Song all by herself. Lots of ladies have collaborated on Academy Award-winning songs, but Melissa is the first to have written that song alone.

It's interesting that her life is so different now after accepting an assignment for which she wasn't paid a dime. She composed it as a favor to a friend, and it certainly came back shining. She has the publishing rights, of course, but was never paid a sync fee for the film. However, there is no amount of money in the world that could create the opportunity of working on a documentary like that with the positive impact it's had on the world.

Melissa is back to touring and promoting her CDs. She performs in venues that hold from 3,000 to 10,000 people. She is cancer-free and very, very happy with her life and her career just the way they are. Her audiences have stuck with her through the highs and lows, and she's very grateful to them. Melissa's wife and four children travel with her in the summer, the only time she tours. And although they don't have a nanny per se, the accountant has a special way with kids and takes care of the children while Melissa is working.

Speaking of working, I asked Melissa about her writing schedule. When she was a kid and unsigned, she wrote every day, she scribbled on every scrap of paper, on the walls if necessary, and ideas were gushing out of her. She wrote them all down. Some of the songs were good, some of the songs weren't, but she kept on writing every day, all day. Now that she's the mother of four, she doesn't have that luxury, but when she has an album to create, she goes into her office, locks the door, and spends time in there each day until the album is complete. If she gets stuck, she takes a shower and usually finds that loosens up the muse. She writes down her appointment time with herself and always sticks to that appointment, no matter what and no matter if the page is still blank from yesterday and the day before. She trusts herself to know that the songs she needs to write are on their way to her, so she has to just keep going and make room for them in her life. The craft of songwriting is very important to her, and her words and music go through many, many drafts before they feel finished. The universe gives her the inspiration to begin the song, but the craftsman is the one who finishes it.

I asked Melissa what advice she has for new writers and singer/songwriters. She said, "I'd play live. A MySpace page isn't enough. It's ridiculous to think that's all you need." Because if she hadn't been performing at Que Sera Sera and other bars those five years, the publisher from A&M, who had previously turned her down, would never have been able to watch her perform, and the A & R person from Island Records would never have seen her, either. She had already tried sending CDs to every label, and everybody had rejected her several times, so being out there in the world made the difference. There's no Internet that can ever replace the one-to-one contact a performer has with his audience.

Recently there was a show on TV about rock 'n' roll moms, and Melissa Etheridge was featured in it. She was singing and playing her guitar. My reaction to her was, "That guitar is not just an instrument, it's a living thing when Melissa plays it!"

I hope you've been to her concerts and seen her perform. I hope you've listened to her CDs, too, especially her latest one, called *The Awakening*. It's good. Very good.

Through this interview, it was exciting to get to know Melissa as a smart, gracious person and a strong survivor of a terrible disease. Through it all she kept on writing.

Each of us has something to learn from that.

Stuff at the Back of the Book

♪ **HOW TO SCHEDULE A PERSONAL, PRIVATE CONSULTATION WITH MOLLY-ANN LEIKIN**

You are invited to schedule a one-on-one consultation with Molly-Ann Leikin to review your work, and, assuming it's ready for the market-place, help you hook up with all the right people. If your material isn't quite ready yet, Molly will give you personal, professional, and very specific feedback on how to tweak what you do so it can realistically compete with the very best songs, bands, and singer/songwriters out there.

You can review her consulting services and professional fees at songmd.com.

♪ **CONTACT MOLLY-ANN LEIKIN**

Residents of the USA and Canada can call Molly at her toll-free number, 800-851-6588. For writers/artists in other countries, you can reach her at: songmd@songmd.com

Please note: Molly works by consultation only. For legal reasons, any material arriving at her office without her consulting fee enclosed, must, regrettably, be discarded immediately. Thank you for respecting the professional parameters of her consultancy.

♪ OTHER CREATIVE STUFF

With the gift of imagination, we can create many magical things, not only songs. Between now and the next edition of this book, I'd like someone to please invent the following:

1. Snap-in replacement vertebrae.
2. Delicious, healthy food that shops for and prepares itself in kitchens that clean up after themselves.
3. Drag-and-drop software to use in moving rain clouds from flooded areas to all the places on earth experiencing drought. It couldn't hurt if this software also had the ability to insert some kind of a whatchacallit into the eye of a hurricane to diffuse it.
4. Candy that has as much protein as broccoli and tastes as good as a Snickers bar.
5. Love that doesn't hurt.

When you come up with any of these, dinner in Montecito is on me.

The Yoga Mat

"The Yoga Mat"
by Molly-Ann Leikin

My precious Jacaranda tree
Drops purple blossoms every spring
On my small quiet garden lawn
A place for peace and pampering

I chase the gardener—Pedro—no!
Don't rake the flowers from that tree
Just let them lie there beautiful
To make a yoga mat for me

I do my ohms and downward dogs
My prayers and meditations, too
And through the windy feathered leaves
I watch our sky that's glory blue

And since I feel such magic here
It has to, has to, come around
That one day while I'm dreaming
All my miracles will flutter down.

© 2008 Molly-Ann Leikin.

For Booba,
because I didn't get a chance
to say good-bye.